PROOF OF
MONEY

The Big Idea Behind Bitcoin

What
You
Don't
Know
About
Why
You
Need
It

TERENCE MICHAEL

100 PERCENT TERRY CLOTH
Los Angeles, CA

Terence Michael/100 Percent Terry Cloth, Inc.

c/o UTA 9336 Civic Center Drive. Beverly Hills, CA/USA 90210

Ordering Information: tman@bitcoinblockbuster.com

Quantity sales. Special discounts are available on quantity purchases by corporations, associations, and others. For details: www.terencemichael.com

Proof of Money: The Big Idea Behind Bitcoin And What You Don't Know About Why You Need It

Terence Michael. —1st ed. 05.12.2023

Library of Congress Control Number: 2023905528

ISBN 979-8-218-15002-0

Contents

Preface

You'll note the book's title is a bold red font set against a black background – not the typical color scheme for a Bitcoin book. Most Bitcoin books tend to display the ubiquitous orange "B" logo against white. It's familiar and eye-catching. It's also friendly and welcoming.

Most books about money or finance trend toward green or blue. Those colors promote growth, stability, and calmness. And for most of the development of the book's design, I stared at mock-ups with a green title.

Conventional color theory states red can induce fear or excitement. I asked ChatGPT what it thought of this color scheme. It told me that red is "associated with warning signs." But it could also convey "importance and a sense of urgency."

Given the current state of global economics, including banking collapses, debt crises, a global recession, infinite money printing, rampant inflation, and a shift away from the U.S. dollar as the international reserve asset, I couldn't think of a better color for the book's cover.

That said, this book is not meant to be read quickly. It's intended to open your mind, provoke reflection, and challenge your views on money.

This book isn't financial advice.

I struggle with this legal disclaimer because Bitcoin's purpose is to free you from the financial constraints of government-created money, especially if you're not aware of these limitations. Bitcoin was designed to empower you to be self-sovereign with your choices and wealth, independent of any authority, company, or state.

However, because our legal system is tied to authority and state, I feel compelled to say: Don't be an idiot (because I might be). Do your homework. Be self-reliant.

The case I make in this book is why I believe everyone in the world should transition to Bitcoin's monetary system. Depending on your unique situation, when, how, and at what rate you do so is up to you and your challenges in the fiat world. This book lays out what I believe is best for me, my family, and friends.

What's best for you is up to you.

If I had my way, I would print the entire book in red. I don't want to scare people away. But Bitcoin is both important and urgent.

I can't think of sharing anything more important than why you absolutely need Bitcoin (but this isn't financial advice).

1
PROOF OF TIME

"This 'telephone' has too many shortcomings to be seriously considered as a means of communication. The device is inherently of no value to us."

Western Union, 1876

An Introduction.

Bitcoin challenges what we think we know about money. It shines a light on money's evolution into darkness and offers a solution to its many shortcomings. For many of the world's problems are downstream from, and a direct cause of, broken money.

Until money is understood and defined, Bitcoin's proposition appears unnecessary. However, once in focus, money leads one to Bitcoin's value.

Like the internet, it's difficult to believe we ever lived without it. What the internet does for information, Bitcoin does for money. It separates it from gatekeepers and opens a world of opportunity previously unknown.

People say money is evil. Its influence can be evil for those who overvalue it when it has undervalued them. The impact of money is evil when a singularity can create or control it at the expense of those who must trade their time for it. The means by which some get or spend it is also evil.

But money is not evil.

Money is merely an agnostic information and communication technology. Like language, it is a trade mechanism. Money allows societies to specialize without physical barter, which is difficult, inconvenient, and inefficient.

It's why we call specific jobs and specialties "trades." When we train our natural abilities and feed our curiosity, we can *trade* that concentrated input for the output of someone else's goods and services.

It's impossible to partition a piece of your farmed cow for the services you need from a shoemaker. That would destroy your farm animal and devalue the remaining utility. What if the shoemaker only seeks a trade with a doctor who can bandage his knee? And what if the only doctor available wants flour to make a cake for her daughter's birthday?

It's a comedy of errors attempting to find a direct match that satisfies both sides of the transaction. One needs a convenience of coincidences, which isn't very convenient.

As information technology, money solves this trade imbalance when it has integrity of energy. Then it can be a promise of coordination.

Without the ability to store time, which is money's primary purpose, we would have to perform a skill to get breakfast. Then again for lunch. And so on. We'd have to "hunt" every day for anything we needed when we needed it.

The incentive structure to shape natural talent would disappear without money. The absurdity and impracticality are so obvious that no one could ever survive. Survival is thus dependent on money's integrity as a conversion tool.

Money is for good, not for evil.

People need an escrow instrument that guards them from loss. They need to save their surplus of resources for future expenditure. We should all benefit when we contribute an excess of our talents into an economy. We added value. We gave society more than we need at this moment.

Past time should be reflected in an increased ability to consume in the future. Without that incentive, why store time?

Consumers, investors, and laborers continue to immunize themselves from the problem. They don't approach money through a first principal lens.

They lack money, encounter rising prices, pay their taxes, and attempt to save or invest. Unfortunately, they aren't where they expected to be, and blame their salary.

They sit in a leaky boat and think a larger bucket is the solution. A larger bucket will get water out of the boat faster. But the solution is to fix the leak. Higher salaries just enlarge the bucket to stay afloat.

All currencies throughout history have deteriorated over time - every single one of them. This makes currency unsuitable for energy retention. This part of money is evil.

When money fails to carry information forward in time, it is no longer money. It may be a currency but not money if it loses energy.

Without options, most have no choice but to define currency as money and money as currency. With perfect money these can be one and the same. But the money that most people are legally required to earn, transact, and pay taxes is currency, not money.

Government-issued currency leaks. It debases. And since money represents your past time, currency devalues your time. It steals worth from you at whatever the inflation rate of that currency is.

How much of your time does that car, that coat, or your electricity bill cost?

Since time is the one thing we all agree is scarce and limited, we place immense value on it. So time is real money, not currency.

We ask the shoemaker what else he might need to meet a trade. Soon we paint the shoemaker's barn even if we dislike painting. But we need our shoes fixed.

If what we love to do can't get us the trades we need, we will perform less desirable functions to get the money to make the trade. And this pretty much sums up how most of the world wakes up and works every day until they die.

The need to make "more money" is a secondary issue. The primary one is that we confuse money with currency. And currency is a battery that drains. Not a great place to value your time.

The breakdown of money goes unnoticed when disguised by those who initialize and control it. The mainstream media perpetuates stories about acceptable inflation levels and the economy's health.

This diverts our attention. We think we need to work harder and make more ice cubes. The problem is our inefficient freezer, not the ice cubes we earn and save.

We attach success and happiness to higher numbers to compromise for this loss of purity. Those numbers become less meaningful as our money supply inflates.

Imperfect and evil money doesn't allow us to holistically do what we want with the tools we have and the experience we gained. Money shouldn't be an obstacle.

Titles and ego are temporary bandages. Labels incentivize us to earn more. But, due to weakening purchasing power, chasing approval distracts us. It works in the short term for people of privileged countries, but decimates most of the developing world under hyperinflation.

Yes, we are oblivious to the problem because scorecards are important.

Everything gets more expensive. Education, housing, gas, food, and health-care rise faster than our salaries. But climbing prices seem reasonable because a higher expense for you is higher revenue on the other side of that trade.

This process is normalized. But it's manipulation of money. It's a coordinated diversion from the real problem.

Inflation is not natural, and it's not necessary.

When prices rise faster than the rate at which we earn, consumption is encouraged over saving. Evil money discourages planning. If everything is cheaper today, we will accumulate disposable stuff now before it gets more expensive tomorrow.

The savings scam is that tomorrow's promise never arrives. Savings for us is leverage for the government's banks to multiply the money supply with loans from our money, not theirs. It negates our savings and decreases our purchasing power. But this dilution of wealth is hidden with a higher quantity of savings.

It's all about purchasing power. We don't really care about money. We care about what money can buy us. An unlimited money supply makes the goods we buy scarce. Prices of those scarce goods rise to correlate to unlimited money.

But a money supply that is limited makes the goods we buy abundant. Prices decline to attract demand for that scarce, valuable money.

Inflation is a stealth tax. Taxpayers won't notice a slow debasement of their currency. But they'll vote people out of office if there's an official tax on the ballot. A government can print more money to pay for its wars and entitlements rather than seek an unpopular vote.

Our children pay for ballooning debt in the form of diluted money, so they need to work harder to get more. They don't need more goods or services than we do. They have the same quantitative and caloric needs.

But they need more of the same currency since more is in circulation. It's a numbers game with the same value recalibrated against higher numbers.

Money can't be fair when it isn't transparent. Without warning, we can't account for or confirm the total money supply when it continues to grow. We can't budget or plan when there's unlimited printer ink.

If there's no denominator on government-created money, how do we calculate our share of the economy?

It's like having the title to one slice of a 5-slice pizza economy. That 1/5th of the pizza is 20% of the network. But if the government re-slices that same pizza to accommodate 10 slices, you suddenly own 1/10th or 10% of the same pizza. You've just been cut in half.

You'll now have to work more to regain the original percentage before the slicing. You go from 1/5th ownership to 1/10th because the government inflates the denominator.

Whereas a stock is a title to a company, money is a title to human time. Thus money is good, not evil.

With corrupt money, our life force has no sovereignty over our choices. Instead, it steals our time and enslaves us. It's why the punishment of choice for most societies is imprisonment.

Because time is scarce (absolute), we don't need to trust it. We all agree and cooperate with the rules of time. There is a fixed supply of time, so no one argues with a clock - ditto for a ruler, tape measure, or any tool we use to coordinate tasks.

But money with an unlimited supply has no universal tool for measurement. Everyone speaks a different language which manifests in paying more.

Have a contractor and subs attempt to build a house with different measuring tools, and that house's cost will skyrocket. No one can coordinate efficiently when a foot declines to 10 inches, then 8 inches, then 4 inches. The price per foot increases as building materials shrink in relation to their measurement.

Money's denominator must be fixed. The numerator - the representation of time and work from holders of that money - should increase. This happens on a Bitcoin standard with a fixed supply of 21 million. Your entire worth is divided by 21 million.

As you work and gain an excess of resources, your worth increases as a percentage of 21 million. Your share of the economy continues to grow. As you peel off money to live or consume, this percentage decreases. But you control and account for this when the money supply is fixed. There's no guesswork.

Bitcoin is a ledger of time. It records value 24/7/365. It captures time around the globe without knowing or caring who the holders are. Everyone can participate in an uneditable and permanent spreadsheet to share and verify for themselves.

Bitcoin is set in time on its time chain (often called a blockchain). And time can't be altered. It prevents money from being altered when money is Bitcoin.

No one can fight the laws and rules of Bitcoin. Like physics, no matter your beliefs, ethics, or personality, you'll fall from the sky at the same speed and velocity as anyone else. The laws of the universe are set in stone and can't be altered by a bad actor who thinks they can fall up rather than down.

Money is proof that work occurred. *Proof of Work* is the culmination of all that energy and effort captured as money - information malfunctions when proof of work isn't present.

We prove we are good parents by raising children who are healthy, happy, and independent.

We prove we have the skills for a job with a certificate or license.

We prove we know with a degree or grades.

Our body proves whether we exercise and eat healthily.

Our pets and plants prove whether we take care of them.

Our relationships prove if we cultivate and support them.

Without proof of work money shifts from a set of rules to a set of rulers. These rulers skew the game in their favor and tell us it's to benefit us all. But each year we play harder and put fewer points on the board.

If we perform work that loses value to imperfect money, that percentage of lost value is wasted energy. We then have to exert more energy to reach an equilibrium of lost value.

Human energy is the catalyst for the consumption of all other energy. When human energy is wasted, so is all generative power necessary to give humans energy in the first place - farming, agriculture, manufacturing, and transportation that provides food, water, and shelter.

Environmentalists often focus downstream on the effects of fossil fuels. But they miss the single point of failure upstream where energy waste begins with inflated money.

How much additional energy are we consuming to counter the debasement of money? When money is corrupt and can't hold value, people will burn tires or trees or whatever they need to provide energy for their families.

Proof of work is wasted when not secured by money with integrity.

Money doesn't start out this way. Every nation-state, every dynasty, empire, kingdom, community, and tribe, since the history of time all across the globe, has started with a predominantly fair choice of money. But as time evolves, we learn in hindsight that it was misused by those who could make more of it.

We evolve to fix these problems by identifying the properties that make honest and fair money. Money changes over time (rulers change over time). And it is changing again at an accelerated pace.

The U.S. dollar isn't going anywhere. It's the strongest currency in the world and will always have utility as a *currency*. But it isn't worth what it was yesterday and won't be worth tomorrow what it is today.

Currency is a hot potato. Devour it or get rid of it. It'll burn you if you hold it too long.

As an international trade, the dollar is already losing dominance as a reserve asset, beginning with those affected most.

El Salvador was the first sovereign country to make Bitcoin legal tender. The Central African Republic was the second country. By the time you read this book, there will probably be several more who have followed.

Both countries are under the oppression of the IMF and World Bank. Both of them have economies consisting primarily of remittances from outside their borders. Both of them are devastated by the inflation of a currency they don't control and can't print their way out of. And both of them have abundant natural resources that favor Bitcoin mining.

The privileged initially view Bitcoin as a shiny object. It's treated as a start-up with potential. Traders flock to Bitcoin at scale with hundreds of millions of people who trade it daily. There is volume and liquidity, and it's bought and sold 24/7 globally in every major currency.

We've never had a tradeable asset that doesn't have business hours, credit risks, intermediaries, executives, bailouts, discrimination, shareholder control, an inflatable supply, customer service, or even a physical address. Having something devoid of these characteristics is entirely alien to traditional finance.

The separation of church and state is heralded as one of our country's most outstanding achievements. Equally important is the separation of money from the state. We interact with money and its representation of our time in everything we do, perhaps more than religion.

Bitcoin is a true and complete separation of money and state. It's impossible to blend the two.

Why can a group of suits (The Fed) with their own agenda alter your time? One printing can diminish the value every single person on our planet holds.

Bitcoin takes time to understand. It takes proof of work. It solves different problems for different people depending on privilege, access, geography and level of censorship.

Bitcoin is a payment and settlement network for some. It is a store of value for others. It's an opt-out from central bank misbehavior. And it is a way to protest without confiscation or sanction.

But Bitcoin is also a genius way to improve the environment. Regardless of your view on climate change, the fact is that Bitcoin aggressively eliminates methane emissions and makes everything it touches carbon negative.

This incentive brings economic prosperity to developing countries that have untapped renewable energy sources but no traditional way to access them.

Remote waterfalls, open oceans near the equator, and sun belts are unfeasible for an energy company to build a grid and delivery system. But Bitcoin miners can drop an isolated shipping container filled with computers and an internet satellite - instant energy.

There is no exhaust, and there are zero emissions from Bitcoin mining. Instead, Bitcoin mining eats the exhaust and emissions of others. It erases those greenhouse gasses from entering the atmosphere in the first place. And it takes no energy away from any other user.

Bitcoin is for the right. It is for the left. It is for the rich and, indeed, for the impoverished. It is many things to many people without taking anything away from anyone else. It is the first money that has no liability to anyone yet benefits everyone.

All assets you have ever "owned" can be confiscated - your house, stocks, cars. And for the less privileged, this occurs without due process. Every single asset you own can be outlawed because they are liabilities.

Bitcoin is the first asset in history that is pure self-possessorship. It is a sovereign property that offers property rights to everyone. It is the first of its kind that we have ever had without any counterparty risk.

Bitcoin ownership requires no state authority or minimum requirement in any measure because it is entirely separate from state.

Only you hold the "keys" to unlock your Bitcoin, which can be nothing more than 12 memorized words.

The misinformed have left Bitcoin with an exchange rather than self-custody. Some have lost entire life savings by placing trust in a third party that rehypothecated their Bitcoin.

But custodians in crypto create the same inherent risks as brokers and banks have in traditional finance. Bitcoin was created to eliminate this trust.

There is no third party or trust required for Bitcoin. It is trustless, which was the missing component of money all this time. It's the need to trust humans that creates money's problems. They often prove to be untrustworthy.

There is Bitcoin the token, and there is Bitcoin the network. Most have a basic understanding of the token, but don't realize it's the network that is most valuable. The network secures, protects, and verifies that transfers of value are accurate without any human intervention.

Wall Street is a multi-trillion dollar industry that mixes and cuts up money into numerous investments and repackages them into Frankenstein products with fancy names to broker for a commission. You need an MBA just to understand them. But they are all derivatives designed to redistribute money from you to them.

Bitcoin introduces a new set of ethical, fair, and moral incentives. And in the process (since I know you're asking), you'll build incredible wealth as a by-product. Basic economics and math favor Bitcoin with a long-term view.

We now sit at the intersection of an antiquated, inferior monetary system and a new, superior one. This brings immense opportunity for those who can adapt and think critically.

This type of transformation has happened with every technology; from libraries to the internet, from dial-up phones to the smartphone, from candles to electricity, from horse-and-carriage to automobiles, from the Catholic church to the printing press, from faxes to PDFs, and from ships to rockets.

The internet dematerialized videos, photos, books, and music into information we could digitally digest. But it left out money.

Digital banks and payment systems are merely debit and credit systems that take several days, have high merchant fees, and aren't accessible to most of the world. In addition, up to 7 or 9 intermediaries need to "talk" during the sequence of money travel from one to another. It requires censorship, permission, trust, and fees.

Bitcoin is the *internet of money*. And like the internet, it is a vast foundation from which unlimited applications can build on top.

When every G-20 nation, the World Bank, the IMF, the SEC, and World Economic Forum; every financial institution, central and commercial bank, hedge fund, asset manager, mutual fund, insurance company; every significant endowment, family office, university, retirement, and pension fund is discussing and debating Bitcoin, you know something is afoot.

You know Bitcoin isn't a Beanie Baby or Rubik's cube when the first question on page 1 of your tax return is, "Do you own Bitcoin?"

That's a lot of energy spent discussing a silly dark-web experiment for magical internet points. That's how critics love to discount Bitcoin. But ask yourself: If Bitcoin isn't here for betterment, why is the entire world adopting it? And why are most governments scared of it yet find the need to be part of it?

Not a single penny is spent in marketing Bitcoin, yet everyone knows about it.

There is no physical product, yet everyone wants it.

No one can flex or show it off, yet everyone accumulates it.

It's private, yet everyone talks about it.

Somehow governors, mayors, congress members, and senators have a need to discuss it. And future elections will be won by those who understand its benefits.

There are a lot of dishonest intellectuals who would rather Bitcoin go away than learn about it. Bitcoin is interdisciplinary. Its branches of influence are abundant.

Bitcoin opens your eyes to monetary theory, economics, finance, game theory, history, software, philosophy, energy, politics, innovation, sociology, privilege, the environment, and critical thinking.

Bitcoin's protocol removes complete and total trust so that 8 billion people, no matter who or where they are, can have a world bank with an untamperable vault stored in their head that is more secure than anything the NSA or CIA can dream up.

The most skilled and talented cryptographers in the world can't break Bitcoin. Those same cryptographers took 30 years to create the mechanics that ultimately formed Bitcoin. Yet, Bitcoin has been here since January 3, 2009 and no one has dented Bitcoin one iota. Bitcoin only gets stronger the more it's challenged.

Bitcoin is the culmination and aggregate of numerous software developments and math breakthroughs over decades that finally came to fruition when the right person(s) selflessly designed it to be its own living, breathing perpetual motion system.

No one else, including Satoshi Nakamoto - the pseudonymous name for the creator of Bitcoin - could ever change, alter, or stop it. This hardening security grows every time a new person joins the network, adding cement on top of cement to increase the density of its immutability.

You might have it good. But this is at the expense of the lion's share of the world who doesn't. We can fix broken money and make it pure and fair in opportunity. Rather than a cost, it's a benefit to you.

But money must be apolitical, permissionless, and decentralized. It must provide verifiable accuracy to anyone and everyone that money can't inflate away.

There is no preferential treatment with perfect money. No one can make more of it, seize it, or taint it. No one is closer to its creation than you or I. It does not rust, melt, or deteriorate. It is portable and infinitely divisible.

And it can transcend space and time, securing your proof of work for generations across oceans or even planets (if we live that long).

Of course, only if the money is perfect.

All are welcome. Bitcoin is voluntary. It doesn't care if you decline. No one else is affected. There is you. And there is Bitcoin. No person, law, nation, jurisdiction, agency, oracle, or entity can come between you and your Bitcoin.

There's an asymmetrical opportunity ahead for anyone who learns about Bitcoin. To ignore it is to ignore the most profound technological revolution we've had since the internet.

If you didn't make millions from the internet's halcyon start-up days in the late 90s, Bitcoin is giving everyone a mulligan. This time around you can invest in the actual "internet," not the companies that were liable to the inflated valuations of their founders.

You can invest in the internet of money while the "Amazon" and "Google" of Bitcoin build on top of it. And you don't have to be an accredited investor, part of a wealth management group, or at an investment bank.

You can be a tribesman in Zimbabwe with a $25 feature phone that doesn't even connect to the internet. That phone will allow you to buy, sell, and transact in Bitcoin.

The auto industry didn't see Tesla coming.

The TV industry didn't see Netflix coming.

The publishing and now consumables industry didn't see Amazon coming.

The music industry didn't see the iPod and YouTube coming.

The hospitality industry didn't see Airbnb coming.

The transportation industry didn't see Uber coming.

Wall Street and central banks didn't see Bitcoin coming.

And some still don't see it. But you see it. It's why you're here.

Let the journey begin.

2

PROOF OF PETRO

"Television won't be able to hold on to any market it captures after the first six months. People will soon get tired of staring at a plywood box every night."

Darryl F. Zanuck, film producer, 1946

The world's reserve currency is the United States dollar (USD). Any significant international trade denominates in our dollars. As a result, USD is the most desired form of savings in almost any country.

It's not that it's the best of the best, but rather the least of the worst.

Only the U.S. enjoys immense financial benefits due to this currency dominance. The most obvious is that we can print as much money as we want at no nominal cost. The actual cost, of course, is time theft.

Other nations would rather their sovereign currency be the global reserve. However, due to losing wars over time, this has evolved.

Spain held the global reserve currency with their gold escudo from 1530 to 1641. Then the Dutch guilder dominated from 1642 to 1720. France followed with their livre from 1720 to 1815. Then the British pound asserted its preeminence from 1815 to 1920.

Today, the USA holds the reserve currency flag with USD. But this power weakens as we near the end of an era of drunken money printing. Like every currency that came before it, The USD is nearing a step down from the international podium.

There has always been (and always will be) a passing of the currency torch from nation to nation. Others resign to, and accept, this standard out of necessity for trade and survival.

There is too much friction to exchange every country's currency with one another. And for lack of any other agreed-upon token, we rely on the strongest currency.

Over the past 50+ years, we've used a petrodollar relationship with countries to enforce our currency's status.

We use oil as a significant source of energy. It generates electricity, heats buildings, and powers vehicles, buses, airplanes, trucks, and ships. It makes plastic, fabric, and fertilizer. Like it or not, we require a lot of oil. And the success of our economy depends on it. That's the "petro" part of the petrodollar.

Now imagine if we could acquire this oil with a currency we can create rather than earn. Poof, there it is. We may be cheating the rest of the world to our benefit.

In 1971 we contracted with most of the Middle East, including the United Arab Emirates, Saudi Arabia, and Qatar, to price and sell their hydrocarbons (oil and gas) in USD rather than their own currencies.

We also included other energy-producing countries like Russia in this petro contract. In exchange, we offered to benefit these countries by selling and training them with our superior military technology.

This arrangement secured our USD by inflating our money supply with U.S treasuries. It basically gave us back the same dollars we spent on importing energy.

This positive feedback loop benefits both parties. Energy sellers get the least inflated currency in the world, USD, but stored in the purchase of U.S. treasury bonds. And we gain the credit, the money from those bonds, to satisfy our voracious appetite for debt.

The petrodollar system gives us the fuel we need to prop up our military-industrial complex to invade third world countries and maintain our access to more oil.

Tanks, jets, missiles, and aircraft carriers don't operate on batteries. They use oil and lots of it, burning over 5 billion gallons of fuel a year. One stealth fighter (which costs $1 billion to build) will expend 16,000 gallons of fuel annually, even when we're not at war. We own hundreds of them.

Any sovereign nation needs to have a military, full stop. But much of it could be scaled back from every militarized country without the need to protect money. Enforcing a country's currency on others outside its borders is why a nation goes to war.

Energy markets are so critical that they influence who holds the currency flag of the world. The U.S. has historically been the largest consumer of oil by far. We consume over 6.5 times more than the next largest consumer, which is China.

It only makes sense that the U.S. would have currency privilege when it is the largest buyer of the largest exports from the largest industry. But China is beginning to surpass us, as we export more of our manufacturing to them. Their labor is cheap. Ours is not (due to inflation).

The oil-producing countries also take the USD they gain to purchase goods and services worldwide. It forces other nations, who want to sell their wares, to trade and save in our USD. This further solidifies the USD's dominance.

But others must work, earn, and trade USD. The U.S. prints it.

We produce these types of relationships to borrow more USD by issuing our bonds. It's all about our bonds.

As the world's largest debtor, at about $32 trillion, we owe more than we will ever pay back because we spend far more than we earn. And our largest expense is the interest on our debt!

Of course, we pay back what we need to by printing more money, not earning more.

For years we have been spending over 100% of our income. Currently, we are spending over 140% of our revenue or GDP (Gross Domestic Product). Imagine making $100k a year and spending $140k every year.

Like a credit card junkie, we cover our nation's interest payments by borrowing more, partly due to this advantageous petrodollar arrangement.

Places like Italy and Greece are worse than ours at 206% and 210% respectively. And Japan is at a staggering 260% Debt-to-GDP ratio. Japan is in imminent danger of defaulting on their currency.

Who would want to save in JGB's (Japanese Government Bonds) when they can save in U.S. treasury bonds? As bad as we inflate, it doesn't come close to most other countries.

The OPEC nations (Organization of the Petroleum Exporting Countries) don't just buy our debt (bonds). They also invest in our assets like real estate and stocks. It inflates the price of investments, giving the illusion of a booming economy. In nominal terms, prices rise and portfolios grow. Consumers gain confidence.

But this price inflation occurs separate from, and without an increase in, productivity. Foreign purchases of our assets don't affect our GDP. There's no new "P." Nothing new is produced into the economy. The same amount of assets and services still exist. There are simply more dollars circulating for the same existing investments. Thus, assets inflate in nominal terms, not value terms.

Drive through any upscale neighborhood near a major U.S. city. Why are so many palatial homes empty? Many are "savings accounts" for foreigners from the top energy-producing countries.

It's estimated that in many parts of New York City and London, 1 in 3 apartments sits empty. Foreigners know we inflate our money supply, in part thanks to them. And as our money supply increases, so do the prices of hard assets.

But there is risk, and foreigners pay close attention. This outright power of the international reserve currency gives the U.S. unadulterated censorship. When everyone is saving and investing in a currency we create and control, it lands in banks or assets we can manipulate.

It is our monetary rail system, not theirs. The rest of the world buys a ticket to ride on our train. So any nation's net worth depends on whether we allow them a seat or kick them off at the next stop. And we don't refund ticket purchases.

The dollar is legal property of the United States. It is rented out for others to use, including ourselves. If we don't pay our rent on those dollars (called "taxes"), the U.S. repossesses our property. And, if the U.S. doesn't like a renter's behavior, it initiates capital controls or confiscation measures.

In February 2022, we canceled Russia, one of the world's largest energy producers. The U.S. and European Union confiscated $630 billion of Russia's reserves held in our banks. Additionally, we cut them off from the SWIFT rail system, which traditional banks use to communicate with each other.

Russia responded to these U.S sanctions and priced their oil in their own ruble for the first time ever. They sold to Germany, India, and China outside the petrodollar arrangement.

Iran followed and priced their oil in yuan for China. And then, Saudi Arabia sold China 25% of their entire oil exports in yuan. All of this happened within weeks of our sanction measures.

China has now been holding more and more of their renminbi currency rather than the U.S. dollar. They don't want their reserves confiscated like Russia. China understands confiscation better than any nation. They are the masters of seizure and surveillance. They systematically close banks and take citizens' entire net worth due to behavior.

This de-dollarization is complicated since China is one of our largest creditors. They hold about 13% or over $4 trillion of our almost $32 trillion debt. When we sanctioned China's ally (Russia), we essentially put China on notice. China knows we can confiscate that $4 trillion of wealth they have sitting in our reserves with the click of a button.

China is our outsourced factory. Rust Belt towns, like Detroit, know this all too well. We have the technology, but China has inexpensive manufacturing (thus considerable demand for oil). We are highly dependent on their imports. Some of this is due to inflation, which encourages consumption, so we buy cheap stuff.

China could in turn sanction the U.S. The U.S. would lose the easy flow of credit to pay its bills and its proclivity for cheap labor and products. It could get the U.S. to manufacture more of its own goods. But it's much easier to create money and buy cheap products abroad than to do the actual work.

Russia's Vladimir Putin may be a psychopathic tyrant. But as a businessman, he dislikes the unfair advantage the U.S. has had with the petrodollar agreement. Can you blame him? He doesn't like to sell his country's greatest asset in a currency that we devalue. And again, we can print it. He has to earn it.

Russia has to produce oil and gas at their cost but then sell it to the world at a value we set.

We effectively tell Russia, "Sell us oil for $100 a barrel. We'll make that $100 worth $80 to you by printing (inflating) 20% more dollars. Thanks for the 20% discount, Mr. Putin."

It's no surprise that Russia now officially allows Bitcoin for monetary trade for any of its industries without restriction. Any nation who wants to trade with Russia can do so with Bitcoin. It is already possible with half-a-dozen other countries, and the number is only increasing as people seek a more fair and neutral form of trade.

It's this unfairness that engenders many of the bad actions of nations in the first place. We too would misbehave if forced to trade in a currency that a competitor could inflate on us to benefit their consumption.

Countries seek alternatives to the petrodollar system that we have benefited from for over half a century. Foreigners can't reliably store in their own currencies due to extreme hyperinflation. So our dollar looks like the best investment in the world compared to theirs.

But if the U.S. can exert outright control and confiscate those saved dollars, it has many rethinking the dollar default as a safe haven.

Wars are about money. This fact subordinates to more noble narratives such as searching for weapons of mass destruction. Nations fight to protect their currency and force trade that will benefit them.

Wars protect our currency, confiscate holders' money, and keep rulers in office. But wars are "good for the economy," so we end up in wars when our economy is bad.

Wars aren't just kinetic with tanks and missiles. Wars are against movements and pandemics.

When the government needs money, there will be a "war" of some kind. It will fire up the money printer in the name of necessity and dig the government out of a hole. But citizens have to work to pay for the shovel.

The fact that wars get financed by citizens is obfuscated by inflation. Because inflation is what pays for the wars. Remember, it's all about the bonds, as in "war bonds."

Most wars would never happen (or end much sooner) if a vote to finance them was required. But by issuing more money into the supply, we create bonds to pay for wars. Thus the costs of goods and services inflate.

The birth of the United States was no different. The British made it illegal for the colonies in America to print money. The British forced Americans to pay taxes and transact with the motherland in the British pound.

We fought and won the Revolutionary War and were then able to establish (and eventually print) our own money. This is why we fight: money.

It's always about money. And more specifically about the fairness of money. Fairness and neutrality are what everyone seeks.

We've had fairness before. But the temptation to cheat never goes away. This is what happens when rulers can manipulate money. They cheat.

3

PROOF OF BREACH

"Rail travel at great speed is not possible because passengers would be unable to breathe and would die of asphyxia."

Dr. Dionysius Lardner, University College London, 1830

Before the petrodollar system of the 1970s, we had another strategy to enforce USD as the worldwide currency. After we won WWII in 1944, The U.S. met with its allies in Bretton Woods, New Hampshire, to solidify the USD's international status.

Everyone from Great Britain to France and Russia to China agreed to trade internationally with each other in one monetary token, USD. But this was strictly conditioned on the U.S. tying USD to gold.

Nations wanted our paper currency backed by *real* money to reduce our unfair advantage of having the international money printer.

And not so coincidentally, it was also here at the Bretton Woods conference that the IMF (International Monetary Fund) was created to promote financial stability among countries.

But for this to happen, USD had to be convertible to gold.

The world wanted the U.S. to play fairly. It was common knowledge that currency was not money. And if everyone were to adopt a singular currency, then it must be backed by actual value, meaning money. Currency is merely a coupon, or an I.O.U., for real money. It is a claim on money, not the money itself.

The agreement defined that any of our foreign friends could redeem a U.S. dollar (the coupon) at our Central Bank and, in return, get a dollar's worth of physical gold (the money). The dollar was nothing more than a receipt for commensurate gold. And that's all it was ever supposed to be.

We have since forgotten this fact, so we confuse currency with actual money.

This dollar-gold peg solved the impracticality of conducting international trade with clunky, heavy metal halfway around the world. More importantly, it held the U.S. accountable for inflating the USD supply. It was a policing mechanism.

The U.S. already held more gold in its reserves than any of our allies after the war, and it was the one commodity that had survived globally for over 5,000 years as an agreed-upon store of value. It had history and time on its side. And no matter what language someone spoke, they recognized gold when they saw it.

Gold evolved as the dominant, defined money, not because any government decreed it into existence but because the people chose it. Holders realized that it held value on its own, independent of state intervention or manipulation.

No government can "make" gold overnight. It requires extensive expense and effort to introduce more gold into the supply. Therefore, it has always been sound, hard money, regardless of religion, culture, politics, or belief.

Alchemists spent centuries attempting to replicate gold. But they couldn't fake it no matter how many chemicals and metals they manipulated to come close to its atomic structure.

In hindsight, counterfeiters should have focused on replicating gold's properties, not gold itself. Because it's not gold that makes gold valuable, it's gold's proof of work.

Bananas could be money if they had the same characteristics as gold. The commodity or collectible makes no difference. It's the properties that matter.

Even so, gold has its limitations. Thus its relationship with a currency is essential. Gold doesn't move like a river or electricity. There's no current. It's heavy.

Shipping gold across the high seas reduces its value due to the costs of security, transportation, energy, and the risk of pirates. Gold can't overcome geography. It is limited in movement due to size and weight. Crossing borders for a single payment in gold could take months, if not years, with proper coordination.

Verifying pure gold is cumbersome and imperfect. There's no universal method that is quick or efficient, especially in global or rural markets.

Some think they can tell by the sound gold makes when you tap it with other metals. Some test it with magnets or see if it floats. Both are imperfect, untrustworthy, and risky at considerable volume.

It takes experts time and precision to validate gold as a natural element on the periodic table, not a fool's gold. Technicians use electronic equipment or perform acid tests with nitric acid.

For total peace of mind, gold must be melted down and solidified again to truly know without a doubt that it is pure gold.

Would you accept gold if a stranger came to your house to buy your car? Gold has been defined as the best money for over 5,000 years by every nation globally. Why wouldn't you accept actual, real money over a receipt for money?

Even nations have been scammed by gold. In 2009 it was discovered that Italian banks were buying millions of dollars of fake gold from a counterfeiting operation. The criminals mixed copper, brass, and other cheaper metals to emulate the look and feel of gold.

In 2013, the Bank of England discovered that the gold they had held in their vaults for over 30 years was counterfeit.

In 2018, the Venezuelan government was using gold as collateral for loans. But it turns out the gold bars the government pledged were all fake. Even after conducting various tests, the gold wasn't detectable as counterfeit. The gold passed the standard tests.

Gold may be technically fungible, as it is a pure element in the earth. 1 ounce is worth 1 ounce. But trust is required of reputable dealers and authenticators to confirm if gold is real. A "normal" person has no absolute way of knowing without trust.

In 1944, we didn't have an invention like Bitcoin to solve problems like these with math rather than trust. In one sense, our allies were looking for this at Bretton Woods. Bitcoin would have prevented any manipulation of any kind and would have provided transparency.

We still had to rely on trust, contracts, and the threat of war. Thus we stayed with the best thing we all agreed on: gold. For all its imperfections, real gold was universally accepted. It required the same of everyone to acquire or earn it (outside of war, that is).

With the Bretton Woods agreement in place, if the U.S. wanted more wealth, it would have to increase its productivity to earn new USD. It would have to perform work. Like our allies, we would have to innovate, crank up manufacturing, and output additional goods and services for consumption.

Suppose we couldn't resist the urge to print money without doing the work. In that case, we'd have to simultaneously get out our picks and axes, don the miner helmets, and go mine gold to collateralize any new supply of USD we added into circulation. We had to retain an equal amount of gold for redemption, so either way, we would have to prove our work.

When it was time to leave the club, countries wanted to present their claim checks and collect their coats. They equally wanted to get their car with a valet ticket. That ticket, without a correlation to the car, is valueless. It's just an expired coupon.

Bretton Woods worked well for almost 30 years. But the U.S. was soon in severe debt, largely due to the Vietnam war. We had actually been spending more than we had by (drum roll)... printing money.

By 1971, our choices were limited. The U.S. government could pay its debts with traditional fiscal tools, like raising taxes, cutting government funding, or both. But austerity measures are unpopular and require votes.

In times of a booming economy, citizens oblige and realize it's prudent. But voters aren't about to approve more personal loss when we come out of a costly, controversial war.

President Nixon also wanted to be re-elected the following year, in 1972. That seemed unlikely if he were to take extra money out of voters' pockets. He had few choices, and the world was watching.

President Franklin D. Roosevelt was in a similar predicament four decades prior as President Nixon. But Roosevelt's advantage over Nixon was that there wasn't an international agreement to tie the dollar to gold.

Within our own U.S. borders, we were already tied to gold. But Roosevelt, like Nixon, needed more money than we had earned without the unpopularity of raising taxes.

In 1933 Roosevelt issued Executive Order 6102. He ordered all Americans to turn gold into the bank. USD would issue as a substitute in gold's place. Anyone caught hoarding gold under their own custody would go to prison.

This process allowed us to stimulate the economy and pay off our debts by printing more money at no cost to the government. But, of course, this was a severe cost to citizens in the form of monetary debasement.

With a divorce from gold, the dollar could run rampant and afford the government anything they wanted. This lasted for over a decade until Bretton Woods in 1944 when we returned to a gold standard.

Other countries also print and depeg their own currency from gold. Although devastating to citizens' sudden decrease in purchasing power, it's an ace card for rulers in the short term. However, the long-term expense has been total ruin, especially for the lower and middle classes who live paycheck to paycheck.

Nations from Venezuela to Argentina, Turkey to Lebanon, and Cuba to Africa have currency that is effectively and quite literally toilet paper. There's a reason almost every single developing nation has extremely wealthy leaders with primarily disadvantaged populations.

This is most of our world, unfortunately, with 130 of our 190 countries classified as developing or "emerging market" countries.

When a nation has sufficiently gained more of their currency via printing, they pay their sovereign debt. Then, they repeg their local currency back to gold, but at a newly inflated level due to its increased supply.

Victims (citizens) of this smoke-and-mirrors tactic are "taxed" without voting for a tax. More paper currency is now required for the same value in gold someone held before the depegging-and-repegging occurrence.

It reminds me of playing video games for a quarter per game as a kid. The arcade required you to use their native tokens. It was their gaming currency. Each quarter bought you one token, so it was a simple 1-to-1 peg. Everyone knew if they were spending a token, it was 25 cents.

One day I returned to discover that the cash machine only spit out 2 tokens per dollar instead of the expected 4. The price of tokens had doubled to 50 cents each. But the arcade advertised that games were still only "1 token each."

You see, they didn't raise prices. They merely inflated the token supply, thus making each token hold less value against the same service, the video game - 100% inflation. Even an 8-year-old can identify the scam.

Nation-states devalue their own people's currency with these same mechanics. Depeg. Print. Repeg. More currency is required to purchase the same goods and services. It's a blatant tax without advertising it as a tax. Political reputations remain intact.

But there's little choice for developing and underprivileged countries who are given loans in USD, often by the IMF or World Bank, and have to pay them back in USD.

Whereas the U.S. can print USD to satisfy its debt, other countries have to export goods and services, often contractually, back to the U.S. They earn USD to pay their debts. We magically materialize it.

This only solidifies the importance of having a currency pegged to real money, or the need to use real money in the first place. Gold could have been money and currency if not for the problems of portability, divisibility, and verification.

But stuck with a currency that is too tempting to use to inflate away debt, President Nixon and the Central Bank decided to detach from gold in 1971. They printed dollars without adding more gold to their reserves and spent like crazy.

There was no additional tax on the people. There was no reduction in spending on politically favored programs. And everyone still conducted business using dollars as they always had. No one had to know.

Except, everyone knew when they wondered why they were having to spend more USD for the same quantity of goods and services. Aha... inflation!

Allies suspected the U.S. was lying and breaking the Bretton Woods agreement. Without proof of work, without an increase in GDP, without proof of mining for more gold, how could the U.S. suddenly have more cash in circulation? Where did it come from?

The world had about $68 billion of gold claims on our reserves. But we only had about $10 billion worth of physical gold on hand. We were re-hypothecating everyone's gold nearly 7 to 1, lending out more USD (because we printed more dollars) against gold than we actually had.

France was the first to send over ships to redeem their gold. Then Germany and Japan prepared for the same. A potential bank run of epic proportions and WWIII may have been near. Thus we started redeeming what gold we could to those first in line. But like a Ponzi scheme, we didn't have enough to go around.

Nixon got on television in 1971 for a special broadcast to head off a worldwide bank-run. He declared that we were officially going off the gold standard. We would no longer redeem gold for dollars. Nixon suppressed international panic and told the world that the backing wasn't necessary because (another drum roll)... we guaranteed it.

The U.S.'s message was that gold didn't give the dollar its value. It was the opposite. It was the dollar that gave gold its value. So it was USD that people wanted all along. Not gold. Brilliant marketing, pure misinformation, and abuse of government power on our wealth.

This abandonment of the convertibility of paper to gold is referred to as the Nixon Shock.

The gold standard was dead. And the government officially defaulted on the world, just as Roosevelt had previously done in 1933. That's 2 defaults within the last 100 years. A third one is coming, especially after the astronomical amount of USD printing from the Covid-19 pandemic (C-19) and bank bailouts of 2023.

After the Nixon Shock, the stock market surprisingly climbed. It went on to gain almost 25%. At first, everyone seemed thrilled because inflation always hides actual costs.

America had increased dollars in circulation by 150%. But economic output grew only 38%. We infused 4 times more currency into a system than the goods and services available. So prices inflated on those goods and services to correlate with the larger supply of USD.

It is no different than what we witnessed coming out of the pandemic that began in 2020. But in 2022 and 2023, prices almost doubled everywhere, and we entered a global recession.

The piper always wants to be paid when the party's over. In 2023 there is over $90 trillion in USD debt. That's the total of all mortgages, credit cards, student loans, fixed liabilities, etc. It doesn't include unfunded liabilities like money owed on pension plans and social security.

But there is only $9 trillion in actual USD. As much as the U.S. has printed, it still only has $1 available for every $10 owed. This is the direct effect of money printing. It puts more money into the system via debt. But it's "air." We don't have it.

Other countries fared much worse. Since the Bretton Woods system ended in 1971, over 220 currency collapses have occurred in other countries.

Because of this reset, a foreigner had to redeem 95% more USD to claim the original amount of gold they had before the Nixon Shock (really, a "Nixon Default"). If they "safely stored" $1,000 worth of gold, they now had to pay $95,000 to get back that same amount.

To further this deceit, no one can accurately confirm or verify how much gold we actually have. Some wonder if Fort Knox may be half empty. Doubtable, but it's interesting to consider why there's no official transparency or accountability.

There has been speculation that while our treasury continues to report that it is acquiring gold, this may be part of a strategic ruse with other countries. Other countries also say they are stock-piling more gold, but no one can confirm it. It might be the most giant poker game ever played.

The Federal Reserve Bank of New York reports over 8,000 tons of gold. If accurate, that still makes us the largest holder of real money.

Germany, Italy, and France reportedly have the next largest caches of gold, collectively owning roughly the same amount we do. Russia is behind them but a close fifth.

London, New York, and Switzerland store most of the world's gold, regardless which country has claim to it. It's inevitable that with future wars this will be a problem.

Gold is easily sanctioned, censored, and confiscated. Many countries are putting trust in these geographies to store their nation's wealth.

Gold isn't honest in a digitally global world. Due to its analog nature, there's no way to verify balances or transfers. It requires so much trust that we have gone to war to debase the value of other people over and over again.

If you can't trust someone, if you can't confirm what they are saying, you fight them. It's always predicated on money. And it's why wars will continue as long as there's debt, inflation, and mistrust in the system.

This unreliability of the paper-gold tether is one reason countries have shifted their focus to Bitcoin. They view Bitcoin as a digital solution to gold's analog limitations. It is odd that in a modern society countries would still base global value on a rock, and one that another country custodies for them.

Bitcoin improves on every quality that gold has and eliminates the inherent flaws previously thought to be unavoidable. It's one reason Bitcoin has been labeled digital gold.

Although Bitcoin is more than just a digital version of gold, it's a fair base-level comparison when considering how one could dematerialize gold and create its digital version. You'd end up with something like Bitcoin.

Without sacrificing the value of their physical counterparts, phone books, maps, libraries, cameras, photos, documents, music, snail mail, alarm clocks, and newspapers have all been converted to digital format.

We value a song or photo on our phone as much as we would on a record player or photo album. Aside from some attached sentimental value to the past, network effects and accessibility have only served to increase utility.

Until the invention of Bitcoin, money had been left behind. Gold was (and is) as archaic as it sounds.

Bitcoin is the missing piece of money. Bitcoin is the digitization of real money. In this respect, Bitcoin has bridged the divide between a solid rock and streaming ones and zeros.

There is, of course, "paper gold," which you might trade in an ETF or buy through a broker. But this is no better than owning currency. Paper gold isn't real gold and is rehypothecated beyond an accurate 1-to-1 correlation to actual gold.

Paper gold is merely a financialized derivative of gold. It is reported (difficult to verify) that there is a 250-to-1 correlation between paper gold and physical gold. That's a scary ratio that effectively inflates the gold supply. Even if the valid number is half that, it almost negates the value of a scarce asset.

It goes for Bitcoin too. It's why you want to own your own Bitcoin with your own keys and not place trust in a third party who might be giving you paper Bitcoin.

We witnessed the effects of paper Bitcoin with the fraudulent operations of Sam Bankman-Fried's FTX exchange. It turned out that his operation didn't own any Bitcoin at all but merely marked people's accounts on a spreadsheet as they bought and sold.

Many think this prevented Bitcoin's price from reaching $100,000 per coin at the end of 2021. It reached $69,000 on November 21, 2021.

Unlike gold, Bitcoin can easily be purchased and sent to your wallet within seconds. This fact will keep exchanges from trading too much paper Bitcoin, as customers will demand their money upfront. And it will keep companies honest when they realize people want to self-custody their Bitcoin.

The minute people purchase Bitcoin on an exchange and can't withdraw it to their own wallet, that exchange will be on notice and won't survive long. Not after the malfeasance we saw with Sam Bankman-Fried and other dishonest operators.

There is also a movement called *Proof of Reserves*, where the Bitcoin community demands that exchanges prove, with wallet addresses, that they hold the Bitcoin they say they have. Proof of reserves is next to impossible with gold since gold isn't digital.

The gold and USD peg has never been restored. So we continue to earn, save and trade a coupon that isn't redeemable for money.

50 years later, we are still operating in this zone of breach. A $10 bill went from reading "Ten Dollars In Gold Coin Payable To The Bearer On Demand" to "Ten Dollars" to "Backed By The Full Faith of The United States Government."

Today, we are backed by "faith." We must trust the entity with unlimited ink and a heavy thumb on the print button.

We are at the precipice of another default with the petrodollar system falling apart. Global inflation is growing exponentially to unsustainable levels. It is higher than it has been in over 43 years. Our government is trying to correct this in the short term, but they can no longer stop it in the long term. They can't afford to. They must inflate. And inflate they will.

For most millennials, inflation has gone straight up their entire lives. They are disadvantaged as a generation by a weaker currency than the one enjoyed by boomers when the money supply was 20 times smaller.

Granted, we are all victims of a supply increase that has only accelerated since 2008, when there was a war on bank implosions (there's that war again to permit us to print).

Since 2008 we've injected $8 trillion more into the money supply. And $6.4 trillion of that came during the 2 years following C-19. That was a 42% increase in our existing money supply in less than 24 months.

The U.S. is losing bidders for its debt as other countries abandon the petrodollar and reclaim their monetary sovereignty with gold, and increasingly with Bitcoin.

We have to buy our debt using Visa to pay Mastercard and Amex to pay Visa. We own nearly $8 trillion of almost $32 trillion in debt. And we won't default on ourselves. Instead, we'll rebrand "default" as inflation, as always.

The BRICS nations—Brazil, Russia, India, China, and South Africa—are moving away from the dollar. Since 2009 these countries have been attempting to escape our dominance. Now that the U.S. has aggressively played its cards with sanctions and surveillance, it is happening.

Argentina, Egypt, Iran, Saudi Arabia, and Turkey are also joining BRICS. Many of the BRICS countries store their wealth (over $5.6 trillion) in our treasury bonds, as well as the Euro, Yen, and GBP.

How long will nations accept devaluation due to inflation?

No matter who adopts Bitcoin first or fastest makes no difference. We will all eventually trade in the fairest token available if we can't force others to trade in our own currency.

Asking people from various cultures, religions, philosophies, and political perspectives to have faith in one another only maintains the lie that they can trust us.

Humans should not have this kind of power over other humans. No matter where we are from or our beliefs, we should not be able to steal human time, which is the definition of slavery.

When this happens, currencies shift, world orders turn, and people seek asylum for truth.

4

PROOF OF FIAT

"The horse is here to stay, but the automobile is only a novelty, a fad."

President of the Michigan Savings Bank, 1903

T oday we still reside on a monetary standard without any tie or correlation to actual money, which began with the Nixon Shock of 1971. It has redefined our currency as *fiat*.

Fiat is the currency a government issues *by decree*. It is forced on the people, not chosen by the people, since it has no backing. In the U.S., it is USD. In England, it is the pound. In Japan, it is the yen. Etc.

Fiat has been weaponized as paper or digital bullets to force behavior even if that behavior disadvantages good actors. Fiat has become a proof of force.

We are forced into USD due to taxes. We can't pay taxes in or ask a merchant to accept gold coins. We can't buy most services with stocks, real estate, silver, or artwork - none are legal tender.

We must convert those assets to fiat to pay taxes or buy goods. But if we sell those assets to acquire the cash to pay taxes, we incur more taxes in the form of capital gains taxes.

Capital gains tax is an enforcement or penalty tax. It's a slap on the wrist (or wallet) for saving in something outside of straight fiat. So we must degrade our value for leaving and returning to fiat.

Fiat is a governmental tool that benefits itself. It allows costly wars to continue, never-ending debt to grow, trade imbalance to impoverish other countries, economic privilege by money creation rather than productive output, and censorship authority if others disagree.

Fiat is unfortunately treated as money by citizens because there isn't a suitable alternative to store monetary energy. However, fiat is only useful as a short-term currency due to its reliance on trust.

Fiat is seamless. It's light, portable, and recognized by everyone cooperating within an economy. Fiat can transcend space quickly via bank wires. USD has the most extensive network effect for transactions of any currency that has ever existed.

Those seeking complete anonymity from their activity want fiat. They want paper cash, not Bitcoin. According to the United Nations, $100 bills are 800 times more likely to be involved in criminal activity than Bitcoin.

Bitcoin is an open, digital spreadsheet that anyone can view and audit. Users can be tracked on the easily accessible ledger. It's not anonymous at all. Private, yes. Anonymous, no.

Critics who continue to say, "Bitcoin is for criminals," don't understand Bitcoin or tools in general.

Belts, cars, hammers, socks, bread, coffee, computers, duct tape, shampoo, gyms, bikes, eggs, baseball bats, and rope are all used by criminals.

Contractors can go without hammers, and sailors can go without rope. And let's get rid of the internet too. 37% of the internet's energy usage is porn. Should we ban the internet?

Cash doesn't reveal where it came from or who held it before you. But with Bitcoin, every single transfer, withdrawal, deposit, purchase, or sale can be traced back to the genesis of that actual Bitcoin when it was first mined into existence and placed onto the Bitcoin ledger for the first time.

Bitcoin's transparency has allowed blockchain forensic specialists to catch scammers and hackers. Almost every Bitcoin exchange has been hacked or compromised at some point. It has nothing to do with Bitcoin, of course. But everything to do with a human-run company that requires (and often breaks) trust.

For this reason, people don't buy groceries and leave them in the basket in the middle of the store. They take them home - ditto for Bitcoin.

Fiat may serve the government, but it incentivizes criminal activity due to its anonymity and the effects of inflation on holders. Since its value depletes, there's a constant need for more.

Conversely, Bitcoin serves the people but encourages morality due to its transparency and effects of deflation on holders. Because its value rises, things become less expensive over time when priced in Bitcoin.

Fiat is fungible. Any $20 is of equal value to any other $20. You'll accept that $20 from anyone, no matter who they are or how dirty the bill is. There aren't grades of value from one bill to the next in terms of spending power, regardless of how old, torn, or stained the bill may be.

Without fungibility each transaction would need to be paused, verified, graded, and given a premium or discount based on the currency's purity. In the digital realm, this issue is moot. It makes fiat highly fungible and effective as currency.

Banks and payment systems mark fiat transactions up and down with accounting debits and credits that reconcile at a later date. Typically, it takes 3 to 5 days for banks and up to a month if a credit card. There are also fees following delays, forms, and fingerprinting for direct wires and transfers.

Bitcoin achieves the same goals as the entire banking and credit industry, but at lightning speed, at no cost, and with the full authority of the owner. No third party or custodian is necessary to make any transaction.

Bitcoin sees no leader, no borders, time zones, politics, wealth, background, race, or status of any kind. The entire reason Western Union and MoneyGram exist is to "help" others circumvent these factors. Never mind the usury fees imposed on those who can least afford it.

No matter how small or large a Bitcoin transaction, its entire value - not a ledger entry, not a temporary credit or debit - moves from point A to point B. It is immutable (unchangeable), verifiable, and permissionless.

The middleman system is to blame for wasted paperwork, time, and energy. Humans need a process of extensive verification and due diligence for only one reason: They don't trust each other.

In the case of real estate, the price for trust is transfer and escrow fees totaling tens of thousands of dollars for one home purchase.

This intermediary process occurs with every fiat transaction we make, just scaled down and sped up for smaller purchases. Two people frequently conduct business at opposing banks. For those banks to communicate with one another, third parties are required.

To balance their budgets, banks borrow money overnight from federal banks. It's a complicated relationship between instant lending and borrowing. Again, due to trust. But this trust adds fees and red tape to everything that could simplify with math.

Even though we have one fiat system of USD for 330 million people in the U.S., there are 50 different sets of rules and regulations due to state borders that delay, charge, inspect, tax, and censor transactions. For a technologically advanced nation, that's a lot of friction simply due to lines drawn in dirt.

How often have you deposited a check only to wait 2 to 3 business days for it to clear? Who benefits during those 48 to 72 hours with your money? Extrapolate this to the trillions of dollars in the banking system that collectively stick in this transaction purgatory.

Banks make piles of cash on arbitrage in overnight markets, lending your money out without your knowledge (unless you read the fine print).

Why are there "business days" in banking in our modern, computerized era? Is a person physically looking at every transfer and deposit and making a subjective human conclusion from Monday to Friday, 9 am to 6 pm?

Bitcoin is entirely friction-free. It can travel from two feet away to the other side of the world without energy loss because it is weightless. There is no disruption or depletion. The absurdly small transaction fee (literally fractions of a penny) compared to fiat is unaffected by distance, amount, or time of day.

Sending and receiving bitcoin requires no infrastructure in terms of personnel, facilities, buildings, or even paper, for that matter. There are no offices. There are no executives, sales associates, customer support, or employees. There is no waste of energy on suits, marble floors, conference rooms, elevator music, or the thermometer displayed outside over a logo.

Bitcoin's validation of transactions is entirely and genuinely decentralized worldwide, where all other users verify whether a transaction is true or false. There is no third party because there are hundreds of thousands of parties who collectively honor truth.

Any bad actor would have to convince hundreds of thousands of people who speak different languages, use different computers, and live in different socio-economic regions, that $2 + 2 = 5$. They will all personally (or automatically) disagree.

It will only change if the incentives of man change and an amendment globally passes that $2 + 2$ no longer equates to 4. Good luck with that.

There will always be convenient services like Visa and Mastercard to aid businesses that don't yet accept Bitcoin directly. These pro-Bitcoin services can connect to almost any Bitcoin account and convert amounts for you automatically. Merchants don't even have to be aware you are spending Bitcoin.

With direct Bitcoin-to-Bitcoin wallets, these conversion and merchant fees are entirely absent. They're peer-to-peer, not peer-to-company-to-peer. Vendors receive their actual money instead of a ledger credit that can be rescinded or challenged.

Those without access to traditional banking services (most of the world, unfortunately), find that using Bitcoin's monetary rails is the most effective way to conduct peer-to-peer transactions without having to pay third-party fees for courier, custody, cash-outs, or payday loan services. There are no bank sign-ups, minimum deposits, or transaction ceilings. Bitcoin is a natural, limited resource, not a business.

Due to trust, Bitcoin will keep disrupting these outdated systems that drain users of time and wealth.

In some countries, citizens must take 2-hour bus rides to wait 2 hours in line to pay a gas bill. Those same people today are using Bitcoin to pay in 2 seconds from anywhere in the world.

Families dependent on remittances from relatives outside their country can receive immediate, total value on Bitcoin's rails without having a bank account, payment app, or even permission. And they don't have to touch Bitcoin. They can hate Bitcoin and still use Bitcoin's financial rails.

If I want to send $10 to someone in Lebanon since their bank has frozen their funds, I can use a Bitcoin payment app that gets them $10 value in their native Lebanese pound within a fraction of a second.

My $10 in USD converts to Bitcoin. That Bitcoin sends to the recipient in Lebanon. If the user chooses, that Bitcoin converts to the Lebanese pound.

Bitcoin transactions happen so instantaneously that the price of Bitcoin is irrelevant. Total value is sent. Total value is received. The choice of currency is up to the recipient.

Much of these faster, smaller payments occur on Bitcoin's second layer. Whereas credit cards and payment apps like Venmo and PayPal are now the second layers for fiat to move it quickly, Bitcoin's *Lightning Network* is Bitcoin's second layer.

Lightning turns Bitcoin into the world's fastest currency by orders of magnitude. Even though Bitcoin is money first, like the internet or iPhone, the apps built on top of its foundation give it further functionality and speed.

I know businesses that outsource their customer service and bookkeeping to workers in the Philippines. The average rate per hour is $1.60. With such a low rate, you hate to see 30% in remittance and transfer fees taken from them, only to receive $1.12. Bitcoin solves this. Right on their phone, they'll receive $1.595 in Bitcoin, USD, or their own Philippine peso.

The fees for Lightning Network payments average around .005 of a penny, regardless if you are sending 2 cents or 2 billion dollars. The amount makes no difference. A typical Visa transaction is about 20 cents, but with another 2.5% of the total transaction amount charged to the merchant.

Bitcoin Lightning is also over 135 times more energy efficient than Visa, using that much less electricity for the same transactions. The code is open-source and free for anyone to inspect, including states, dictators, or any three-letter agency.

To the 5 billion people who either don't have bank access, are blocked from Venmo or PayPal, are forbidden to use Mastercard or Visa, receive remittances in other currencies from other jurisdictions, or are censored in one form or another from value transfer, this is a game-changer.

Even here in the U.S., we can't send money to people in Crimea, Cuba, Iran, Sudan, North Korea, or Syria, and vice versa. Political sanctions may be warranted, but what about trapped citizens? Good people in these regions are completely cut off from relatives' support in America.

Places like Argentina, Turkey, and Venezuela inflate their citizens' currencies into oblivion. Bitcoin is the escape hatch for them. It's an alternative monetary system by and for the people. Bitcoin's lightning payments allow them to transact daily on monetary rails without inflation. They can buy, sell, save, transfer, and make payments without confiscation or torture.

From September 2021 to 2022, when tensions were high in Russia, Ukraine, Lebanon, and even Canada (trucker protests), Bitcoin's network settled over $50 trillion. By comparison, Visa did $13 trillion during that same period.

A large part of this discrepancy is that Bitcoin offers access to 8 billion people worldwide 24/7/365, along with separation from state control.

Visa is available in many parts of the world but still accounts for under 800 million people, 1/10th of the global population.

Those are the privileged ones like you and me. We were permissioned after an application, identification, and credit check.

Legacy institutions like Morgan Stanley have said Bitcoin's network is more efficient, practical, and economical than debit cards. You can hate Bitcoin for whatever reason you want to, but you can't deny the technology. It is why Bitcoin's network is so valuable, even if you never want to own Bitcoin.

The first layer of the Bitcoin network batches all transactions into 10-minute blocks. Like a bus that shows up at a stop every 10 minutes, passengers must wait for the bus and then pile in. But each bus only takes 2,000 passengers (2,000 transactions). This slower speed is what allows the egalitarian decentralization of its users.

Due to the stable speed, any Bitcoin user with a standard laptop will have enough capacity and hard drive space to monitor these blocks. Any higher degree of activity could prevent participation from "normal" people.

Fundamentally, the internet could be faster. Remember dial-up? Remember cat photos taking 30 seconds to load? That late 60s technology that birthed the internet has stayed the same since it surfaced. But http and websites were built on top as fast, secondary layers, just like the Lightning Network on Bitcoin.

Now, over 5 decades later, you can stream a movie on what was originally a military and academic mailing system.

Browsers and apps didn't start their own version of the internet to compete with the original internet. They offered services on top of the solid and proven internet to take advantage of its network effects and stable foundation.

Some cryptocurrency projects like Cardano, Solana, or Ripple can settle payments on their own protocols in seconds. The technology and speed are impressive. However, those projects use their native tokens (not Bitcoin). They aren't moving any *money* whatsoever.

Bitcoin transactions move actual money, not a token without a fixed supply, and not a credit or debit for later settlement.

Since there is no issuer or counterparty of Bitcoin, it is 100% owned and controlled by the person who has it until the next person has it. No one comes between those two parties, especially a company with investors.

Bitcoin doesn't solve speed. Speed isn't a critical problem for money. The issue is decentralization and freedom from manipulation by any hierarchy. Bitcoin is about security and stability. It is willing to sacrifice speed for those qualities.

But even at a limit of 2,000 transactions per 10-minute block, Bitcoin has no limit to how large a transaction can be. A single transaction can be a user's internal batch of $100 billion if they choose.

Users can still transact above Bitcoin's base layer with lightning-fast speeds and unlimited transactions, only to settle on the base layer when it's time to pay the bar tab.

Part of the problem is the word "cryptocurrency." Bitcoin was unfortunately labeled early on as a "cryptocurrency" by mainstream media and journalists. But just because they call it that doesn't make it so.

Satoshi Nakamoto, the creator of Bitcoin, never once used the word "cryptocurrency" in his original 8-page white paper.

Is Bitcoin cryptographic? Yes. Is it a currency? No, it is money. But Bitcoin can efficiently work as a currency because of its second layer where apps empower useability.

It's like asking if the internet is a theater. No. It's a decentralized information tool. But apps and companies can build on top, on a second layer, and make it a theater.

When Bitcoin rises in market price, users feel confident and start gambling with cryptocurrencies. When Bitcoin declines in price, they sell out of cryptocurrencies and jump into Bitcoin.

Every 4 years, we hear about another two dozen altcoins. And every 4 years, most of those become dust in a wallet. Over 90% of all altcoins trend to zero within these 4-year time frames due to Bitcoin's somewhat typical bull and bear cycles.

Altcoins serve as "currencies" for their insular ecosystems. The creators and their investors make overall project decisions, influence the price, sell to fund further development and make changes with votes that they control.

The SEC has defined these cryptocurrencies as securities because, like stocks, which are securities, they have the same risks. They begin with the intention of profit.

A security is an investment. Good or bad, as an "investment," it needs to be regulated and treated as such. It isn't money. This is the distinction. A security is a business structure.

Stocks and cryptocurrencies are pre-funded by founders and investors who give themselves shares (stocks or tokens) before the public. With stocks, there are IPOs (initial public offerings), and with cryptocurrencies, there are ICOs (initial coin offerings).

It's the "initial" part of the IPO or ICO that defines them as securities. They are businesses that favor their founders and investors, not the public. This is legal and acceptable. But it is not money.

If you want to own Ethereum's ETH token, investors should know that 70% of its original supply was given to its original foundation of engineers and coders. You, however, have to pay for the same token.

If you want to own Solana's SOL token, investors should know that it has shut down 10 times and had to be "rebooted" by engineers.

The SEC's chairman, Gary Gensler, said in an interview with New York Magazine:

"Everything other than Bitcoin, you can find a website, you can find a group of entrepreneurs, they might set up their legal entities in a tax haven offshore, they might have a foundation, they might lawyer it up to try to arbitrage and make it hard jurisdictionally or so forth.

They might drop their tokens overseas at first and contend or pretend that it's going to take six months before they come back to the U.S. Still, at the core, these tokens are securities because there's a group in the middle, and the public is anticipating profits based on that group."

Bitcoin never had an ICO or advantage of any free coins, even to Satoshi himself.

To jumpstart the issuance of Bitcoin into the supply, Satoshi mined about 1 million Bitcoin. But that Bitcoin has never once moved from those wallets going back to 2009.

Satoshi knew that gaining any initial privilege to Bitcoin would defeat the purpose of Bitcoin. He either threw the keys away or died with them, making the ultimate sacrifice and donation to the network (making Bitcoin even more scarce).

Bitcoin is a man-made system released by that "man" into the world as a system as secure and unbreakable as physics, math, or language. It's now a law of nature. And the laws of nature are the only rules man has never been able to break. He has broken all other laws.

Altcoins need to register with the SEC. But since most of them haven't, or can't (in all fairness, the SEC makes it difficult), they pump-and-dump on holders from offshore exchanges to get in and out with their Ponzi scheme.

Those who are well-funded and attempt to play by the rules get sued by the SEC, settle for hefty penalties, and continue to operate until the next lawsuit.

The 22,000+ altcoins that have existed are all securities. Every one of them has hijacked Bitcoin's definition of "decentralization." You can't have decentralization if there's a company making decisions or issuing coins. By definition, that makes the network centralized.

Had cryptocurrencies never surfaced after Bitcoin, calling Bitcoin a "cryptocurrency" may have stuck. But for the same reason, you wouldn't call a human an animal (even though they may technically be), you wouldn't call Bitcoin a cryptocurrency compared to how they operate.

Bitcoiners cringe at the word "crypto" for this reason.

There were about 800 cryptocurrencies established in 2014, 5 years after Bitcoin. Of those, 550 are now dead and no longer in circulation. You can't sell or even access those if you still own them. In 2017, this number grew to over 700 dead altcoins. And as of now, over 90% of all altcoins ever in existence are gone or delisted from public access.

Altcoins allow those with money and influence to own the vote of their protocol. No one has to prove their work, like Bitcoin. They only have to put up money to censor and make decisions for the majority. Anyone can buy "proof" if they put up the "stake."

This is why most cryptocurrencies operate on *Proof of Stake*. It's a simple system where you stake money rather than prove your work. That stake allows the "stake" to vote for change.

Votes don't tie to users but rather the amount of money staked. It's pay-to-play. Those with enough wealth can halt transactions, reverse transactions, sanction users, freeze funds, print more tokens, kick users off, etc.

Bitcoin operates on a *Proof of Work* system, which ties energy and effort in the real analog world to the digital world. It's not printed out of thin air like fiat. Instead it is mined through a process like gold.

Due to proof of work, Bitcoin is legally defined as a commodity, not a security, by the SEC. A commodity is an asset without an issuer. There is no company behind its existence. Complete ownership is proven merely by possession of it. It is legal property without liability on the other side.

I don't have a problem with altcoins. I'm in favor of capitalism and entrepreneurship. Let people, start-ups, and investors create and do what they want. Systems (including humans) must fail on their way to learning and discovery.

Most hard-core Bitcoiners once started with and traded altcoins. They, too, had to learn the difference.

I have an issue when the public confuses Bitcoin and "crypto" as one and the same. Newer users get distracted by shiny objects. Bitcoin isn't shiny. It's boring. But money should be boring. It's just a tool.

For money, there is Bitcoin. For gambling, there is crypto. Eventually, everyone ends up with Bitcoin. It's a matter of if they do it the boring way and start with it, or crawl there after losing their shirt with crypto.

With Bitcoin, you own the internet of tomorrow. You don't have to gamble on altcoins or cryptocurrencies. That only distracts from the importance of Bitcoin and what it provides for 8 billion people.

When it comes to "people's money," the point of moving toward a more fair and honest system is to have one that no one over another can sway.

Altcoins do not solve the fiat problem. They simply replicate and transfer it to their own blockchain. They become their own Federal Reserve. They become their own central bank. It only exacerbates the problem.

With Bitcoin, there is no authority. No rulers. No politics. No power structure. No hierarchy. No ranking. No investors. No lawyers. No pitch decks. No seed rounds. No bank debt. No shareholders. No board meetings. No alliances. No influence. No backchannels. No strategy. No privacy policy. And no special treatment. That is Bitcoin.

Crypto is the opposite of every one of those sentences above.

Again, Bitcoin is not crypto.

In time, Bitcoin will be a universal medium of exchange. Until then, discounting Bitcoin because less people currently conduct business in it, is a mistake. It's like ignoring a big block of valuable gold because you can't buy a coffee with it. That's not the purpose of gold. And it's not the purpose of Bitcoin.

5

PROOF OF MATH

"The wireless music box [radio] has no imaginable commercial value. Who would pay for a message sent to nobody in particular?"

David Sarnoff's associates urging him not to invest in the radio, 1920 (he founded RCA Records)

W e have paper USD like the $1 bill, $5 bill, or the $20 bill. And, of course, coins. They all add up and divide into acceptable units based on math. USD is a solid *unit of account*.

No one in the world will argue that five $1 bills are not equal to one $5 bill.

With fiat, consumers can transact confidently and without concern that the retailer will only accept bird feathers as payment. In the past, some kingdoms or regions used other collectibles or commodities as money. For some, sheep was their unit of account.

Everything, whether a horse, a house, or a bucket of corn, would be priced by how many sheep it equaled. But not everyone wanted to raise and store sheep. They wanted to transact in their own choice of money.

Regardless of the accepted technology as money, its parts must equal the total sum. And the total sum has to be equal to its parts. Otherwise, it isn't money.

For example, real estate doesn't work as money. The total sum of a house is greater than the parts. If you break down a house and sell the wood, the tile, the doors, etc., you wouldn't get anywhere near the total sum for the completed house.

Sheep had the same problem. 4 legs, a body, and a head are worth less in aggregate than the identical quantity of a complete sheep.

Because gold is based on a weight system, it is measurably divisible and acceptable as parts. Ten 1 oz coins are as satisfactory as one 10 oz bar. But the time it took to melt down and pour into appropriate fractions was (and is) impractical for most transactions.

Consumers will naturally gravitate, whether cognizant or not, to a token that is most fair. The forces that disrupt this tendency are ones from authority, like fiat.

Bitcoin has the potential to become the ultimate unit of account. It can fractionalize to a greater degree than any money or currency before it. And the sum of its parts is equal whether separated or combined. There is no discount or premium if it is fractionalized or not.

Bitcoin is essentially infinitely divisible. There are precisely 21 million Bitcoin tokens on the Bitcoin network. These "coins" can be divided into

100 million pieces known as "Satoshis." It indicates that the total supply of Bitcoin is 2.1 quadrillion units. Or 2,100,000,000,000,000 Satoshis.

If each of the 8 billion people on the planet were to acquire Bitcoin equally, no person could have more than 262,500 Satoshis (colloquially referred to as "Sats"). If Bitcoin prices at $100,000, then each person could have an equal share of 262,500 Sats for $262.50.

Rarely will you ever transact in a whole Bitcoin.

A single Bitcoin can compare to a bar of gold. Most of the gold bars you have seen in cartoons or movies are 400-ounce "bricks." So at $2,000 per ounce, for example, a gold bar costs $800,000. You will make few, if any, transactions with that much gold or carry it with you to see a movie.

In contrast to gold, Bitcoin can be stored safely and fractionalized to enable instantaneous transactions simultaneously, all without letting on how much money you have. You can spend 25 cents but travel with $100 billion worth of Bitcoin in the same wallet. It is no less secure or more revealing. This can't be accomplished with gold.

How do you get on an airplane or buy food from a taco truck and hide your wealth simultaneously? It is impossible with every money technology we've ever had until Bitcoin.

Sure, fiat will allow you to make purchases anywhere. But remember, fiat is not money. You are not retaining your spending ability in the future if your wealth is held in fiat.

Your bank, Visa, PayPal, Swift, etc., know exactly how much money you have. They also need your personal information to buy that taco. Why do they need to know where you live, your phone number, and your credit score to buy a taco?

Any two Bitcoin users can transact with each other without ambiguity. The Bitcoin network's only job is to make sure that there is never more than 21 million total Bitcoin in the network, and that once Bitcoin transacts, it records where it came from and where it went. That history remains on the ledger forever.

Since there are 100 million Satoshis in one Bitcoin, if Bitcoin's market price is $100,000, then each Satoshi is 1/100th of a penny. One will never need a fraction so small to transact. So why is it so highly divisible?

Satoshi Nakamoto wanted to accommodate an eternally rising Bitcoin price. Because of Bitcoin's fixed supply, he knew it could increase forever when priced in inflationary fiat. In his original white paper, he wrote, "It might make sense to get some in case it catches on."

Thus Satoshi had to make the units unfathomably small to accommodate its eventual rise. When Bitcoin reaches a price of $1 million (I suspect this will occur around 2033), 1 Satoshi will equate to 1 penny. And you might have a transaction where you need 1 penny's worth.

Although pennies today appear to have no value, Bitcoin enables the aggregate value of the crowd to transfer with micropayments in novel ways. You can donate 2 cents to someone if you like their tweet, article, podcast, or YouTube video.

Imagine sending 3 cents to an artist in Argentina. Within milliseconds you can transfer that full value directly to her without a fee. It can be Bitcoin, USD, or her native currency. It sounds small, but extrapolate this to the crowd, and this artist is paying her bills by opening a new portal for micropayments.

Are you willing to accept a cost of 1 penny for every email you send? What if I told you we could eliminate 90% of email spam by adopting that as a standard? It could also curtail the excessive emails some lazily send back and forth without thinking first.

Or what about an article you want to read that has a paywall? To read that one article, you have to sign-up, reveal your name, indicate where you live, and provide other personal identification. Once again, it's too much information that shouldn't be necessary for money.

A platform could make more money if they allow micro Bitcoin payments of Satoshis to access one-offs, rather than having to subscribe and cancel 30 days later. I'd happily pay 10 cents to read an article but not $8.99 monthly for yet another subscription.

With Bitcoin, the value is the value. You don't need to confirm your identity because the transaction is irreversible. A company doesn't need to come after you. Once the platform receives your Satoshis, it's a final settlement. They have it. You can't later rescind the transaction or say it wasn't you. Only you can send it; no one else.

Fiat is credit. It isn't money. It is still a coupon for gold but without the gold. Because of this, we have all of these protocols to protect merchants and payment services.

Final settlement doesn't occur at the transaction level with fiat. So you better reveal where you live so vendors can show up at your door if you don't pay for that taco in 30 days.

Bitcoin is the final settlement. It is money.

Because fiat is credit, it will never be efficient for micropayments. Accommodating such small transactions takes too much time, effort, and fees.

However, micropayments with Bitcoin promote appreciation. More people can contribute to charity when it's 6 cents here or 10 cents there. It sounds insignificant but adds up, especially in regions where a few USD will purchase a day's food.

A vast portion of the global economy is cut off from opportunity due to the lack of micropayments. When fees exceed the actual payment, no one thinks of sending it. But if you could push a button on your phone and send 5 cents to each of 100 different people in one day, you'd make the day for 100 other people in the world. And it costs you 5 bucks.

This is the whole point of Bitcoin as sovereign money: no permission and no friction with fees or intermediaries. You can avoid the nonsense of all that identification required to "protect" your money and thus limit your ability to transfer value.

However, money's requirement to store value is more important than any of this. Money must be a store of value if nothing else (and above all else). It is the most crucial characteristic that defines something as money.

It's essential to be able to send $100 3,000 miles away. But it's more important to be able to send $100 3,000 *days* away. Money must hold financial integrity across time with zero loss of stored energy.

If money can't retain and carry its originally captured value forward in time it is not money. It is theft.

Money does not have to be a *medium of exchange*. It can be, as Bitcoin can. But like gold, it doesn't have to be. Only currency has to be a medium of exchange.

Money, however, must be a *unit of account* and a *store of value*. Bitcoin meets both criteria exponentially more than anything that came before it.

Without stored value, the unit of account is meaningless. It is corrupt because it bases accounting on a supply that keeps increasing. You can't calculate accurate value with a growing denominator. This kills the "account" part of the unit of account.

And without stored value, trade decisions are made using fluctuating metrics instead of fixed logic, corrupting the exchange medium. The medium becomes unstable, which hinders fair exchange in a marketplace.

If you only need to spend 1 hour of an 8-hour work-day to cover that day's expenses, the money token must preserve those unspent 7 hours of work. Those 7 hours of life force are time you gave up to do anything else so that you can eventually trade those 7 hours for other goods and services.

Otherwise, your time is devalued due to energy decay, and there's no need to contribute excess energy to society. Just perform the bare minimum to get by when you need to.

If you make a large purchase requiring multiple months or even years of your past time, you transfer all that past hard work, stress, and energy into the purchase. That purchase now represents the compression of all those months and years of "sweat" you exerted to acquire this purchase. You don't take this lightly. You responsibly scrutinize because it represents so much of your past life force. And you value that.

The first law of thermodynamics says that energy can't be created or destroyed. Energy can only transfer from one form to another. Energy conserves because it remains constant over time.

Thus monetary energy is the conservation of value. It transfers your value into a service or good and then back to you when you sell or leverage the utility from that service or good.

To accept anything less than an impenetrable, airtight financial container is to break the law of energy. It corrupts and distorts your time, which is energy. It takes what you sacrificed in the past and edits your 1 hour of work down to 55 minutes of work, and then to 50 minutes of work, and so on.

In hindsight, you worked way less than you thought if the math measuring your time breaks down. It is equivalent to accepting less money than you charged for your services. It's the same as receiving a lower salary than you negotiated. It's the same as selling your goods, assets, or products for less than you thought you did.

Until we sit down and think about this, we will never understand inflation's evil effects on our time. Our only representation of our past time is what that time produced for us. And anything we didn't immediately trade for that time gets stored into money.

If money loses integrity, it is no longer money. It is currency. It is fiat. It is theft.

This is the big idea with money. It is the raison d'etre for Bitcoin: store of value.

It wasn't as big of a problem when currency was backed by gold, thus defined as money. You could save and hold your worth simply in the convenience and ubiquity of dollars. Many never got the memo that this changed after 1971, and then they wondered why everything was so expensive.

At the time, gold was a more perfect form of money than anything before it. However, gold has never been able to transfer its value across borders efficiently. Even in our modern era, there has never been an easy way to deal with physicality and weight that cannot be collapsed or hidden.

Within certain geographical boundaries, gold will undoubtedly endure indefinitely. Gold doesn't deteriorate or age. It is inert. And like energy, gold doesn't disappear. It simply transfers from one form to another.

Today there is the same quantity of gold on earth as ever. It simply gets remelted and transformed into various artifacts, such as coins, bars, jewelry, and so on. It can't dissipate or disappear.

If physical location isn't an issue, gold is hard and sound money for its ability to store value within that contained area. But because economics is global, the value is affected by its limitations to move value across space.

We have already mined the gold that is easily accessible near the surface. Going deeper into the ground and using more expensive equipment is required to obtain more gold.

At levels that matter, gold mining needs permission. The environmental impact caused by the mining process necessitates extensive political and centralized approval and regulation before excavation can begin in almost any country.

There is typically a multi-year timeline from when the search, identification, and excavation of gold begins to its final form as bank-grade quality. It is limited and difficult to obtain. It requires immense proof of work.

Gold is so difficult to mine, yet deemed valuable enough for the effort, that average individuals go poor trying to "pan for gold" to find flakes here and there that may barely cover their expenses. And that's if they find it.

Gold has averaged a somewhat steady 2% inflation of its supply yearly, much better than fiat's astronomical supply increases. But this 2% inflation can change with discoveries, innovation, or research.

As technology advances or the price of gold goes up, more resources will funnel to find even more gold and at a faster pace. The gold supply will be so large that the price will plummet. Thus gold's supply, although limited, is only limited to the time, energy, and investment one is willing to put in to bring more into the supply.

The barrier to entry is also so great that it's often only governments or large public companies that can introduce gold into the circulating supply.

Even though gold's supply is limited to what is on earth, no one is exactly sure how large that supply might be. It's like saying that grains of sand are limited. Yes, but can we not find more in the ocean?

We just don't know if there won't be a gold discovery that suddenly inflates the entire market. We don't know if an asteroid, however remote this might be, lands on earth filled with gold.

In June 2022, Uganda announced the country had discovered 31 million metric tons of gold. They could produce over 320,000 tons of refined gold, worth $12 trillion on the open market.

Without an issuance schedule of when and at what rate this gold will surface, it can inflate its supply by 185%! It's one thing to experience this level of hyperinflation on an asset you store your wealth. It's another not to be able to plan for it.

Elon Musk has joked that he'll send mining equipment into space to mine gold off other planets and bring it back. He also used to joke about self-driving cars, flying people into space, boring tunnels underground, and having internet satellite connections from anywhere in the world.

For example, there's an asteroid right now that sits between Mars and Jupiter. Some gold miners (including Elon Musk) have their eyes on it. It is estimated to contain roughly $700 quintillion worth of gold. That would give every human on earth over $100 billion. It would hyperinflate gold into oblivion, making it worthless or as much as a grain of sand.

Bitcoin takes the hardness and durability of gold to transcend time and adds to it the ability to transcend space. It can do this because, unlike gold, Bitcoin has a verifiable and finite supply.

More Bitcoin cannot be introduced via a discovery, large investment, or updated technology. It makes no difference how high Bitcoin's market price rises. The supply will always be at most 21 million Bitcoin.

Unlike gold, Bitcoin's total supply was released all at once on day one. All 21 million of it can be seen locked in the code on Bitcoin's blockchain. But to introduce Bitcoin into the circulating supply (Bitcoin accessible to users), there is a precise, programmable issuance rate.

The Bitcoin network started running on January 3, 2009, with an issuance rate of 50 Bitcoins every 10 minutes. Like a faucet dripping water from a fixed water tank for the first time, Bitcoin's network dripped these 50 Bitcoins into the first block.

Then after 10 minutes, the next block filled up with another 50 Bitcoins. And so on. These 10-minute blocks have never stopped and are still going today.

Each time a block receives new Bitcoins from the "water tank," that tank decreases by that amount, thus maintaining 21 million Bitcoin, whether accessible or not.

The number of Bitcoin entering each block shrinks as time goes on. In 2012 this issuance rate of Bitcoin was cut in half to 25 new Bitcoins every 10 minutes. Drip. Drip. Drip. Drip.

Then in 2016, this was halved again to 12.5 new Bitcoins. Drip. Drip. Drip.

Then in 2020, the new Bitcoin was reduced by half again to 6.25. Drip. Drip.

The faucet keeps tightening, so the rate of new Bitcoin that enters the supply slows down to a trickle.

After May 2024, 3.125 Bitcoin is introduced into the circulating supply with each 10-minute block. Drip.

This "Halving," as it's known, takes place roughly every four years, exactly as coded, to resemble the escalating difficulty of mining new gold.

With this halving process, Bitcoin's available supply avoids inflation and becomes *deflationary* due to lost or inaccessible Bitcoin wallets.

All 21 million Bitcoin are on the blockchain. But those losing access to their Bitcoin can never touch it. And thus, Bitcoin becomes deflationary, reducing the amount of Bitcoin that can ever be spent or sold.

The price of Bitcoin would increase from these halving events alone if demand for it never rose. We've seen this happen after every single halving event, as scarcity drives market price.

No halving event has ever had a lower Bitcoin price than the prior one. Pay attention, investors!

Bitcoin purchased within a 4-year time-frame (the distance between halvings) has never lost money. Period. Again, pay attention.

In a shorter time frame, Bitcoin's price fluctuates wildly. We've had numerous drops of over 80% in price. But every single time, and typically around 6 months after a new halving, Bitcoin has recovered in market price.

Gold is a 5,000-year-old asset yet has never exceeded the $2,000'ish range for very long. If the gold price suddenly pops up to $4,000, mining companies will dig in, literally, and bring more gold into the available supply. It will simply drive its price back down. It's all about scarcity.

Bitcoin is the first money in history where its total supply is utterly unaffected by an increase in demand.

The faucet that drips Bitcoin is always turning tighter and tighter. Nothing can or ever will change that. Mining can improve. Technology can improve. The price can explode to $2 million per coin. Bitcoin's issuance and total supply will forever remain the same. Drip.

Bitcoin has become better gold than gold.

Remember, the properties of gold make it hard money, not the gold itself. But for every quality gold has, there are flaws, whether in portability, verifiability, issuance, etc.

These are all solid qualities, but not without limitations that diminish gold's value. Bitcoin has eliminated these flaws and perfected the qualities gold seeks. Bitcoin is the solution that alchemists couldn't find.

The tiny trickle of Bitcoin into the circulating supply will eventually be so small that we will finally reach the 21 millionth Bitcoin in the year 2140. You and I won't be around. But our future generations will. And they'll be thankful we picked up some Bitcoin when it was cheaper than $2 million per coin.

Anyone can confirm Bitcoin's supply, issuance, schedule, and halvings. It is all programmatically fixed and secured by math. The code is open-source for every engineer, programmer, or average smartphone user to stress-test and verify its simplicity and honesty.

Now compare Bitcoin's issuance to that of fiat.

Fiat's issuance is unknown, unlimited, and unsupervised. It gushes from a pipe that cranks open as time goes on rather than shuts. And only a few get to stand under that fiat flow and capture it, namely governments, dictators, large corporations, politicians, and those closest to the printer.

6
PROOF OF SLAVERY

"Who the hell wants to hear actors talk?"

H. M. Warner, Warner Brothers, 1927

A flaw we've normalized is that we can save in a currency system with an unlimited supply. This is fiat's greatest downfall.

It's discriminatory to have a government control and authorize money in the first place. And it's unethical to allow them to make as much of it as they want.

This debauchery occurs because there is no cost to creating fiat.

Money must cost more to produce than it is to earn to disincentivize counterfeiting. It's the only reason counterfeiters exist. If bad actors can create money for less energy or cost than a contribution to the economy, they will.

I'm referring, of course, to governments and central banks.

Easy money creation destroys the pursuit of specialization and expertise. Integrity in an economic ecosystem is lost if focus shifts to money rather than societal output.

Money must be the means, not the end.

Over 55 global hyperinflations since the 1920s have completely decimated the wealth of sovereign nations. These are the consequences of an infinite supply with a chosen money token that is too easy to create.

A government can collect taxes, build infrastructure, and roads, pay for programs, educate, and defend its borders. It can honor votes and elections, allocate money, and budget accordingly.

Even a 5th grader understands the concept of budgeting an allowance. But banks violate this elementary restraint. They gaslight citizens into thinking it is customary to pour newly materialized money into a system via a funnel where only a few at the top capture most of the benefit.

When the U.S. Central Bank (the Federal Reserve) injects more money into the supply, it doesn't pour evenly over taxpayers. Instead, it funnels down a set of stairs where those on the top stair receive most of the benefit, and those on the bottom stair receive little value.

The recipient with the most leverage and benefit is the government itself. It prints in the first place to pay its debt. It is always for a "war" against something, which helps justify the inflation it creates.

Next, the newly created money flows down to Wall Street, investment banks, and mega-corporations in political alignment with the government.

It sells as infrastructure rebuilding, economic stimulation, etc. That may be true in the short term, but it compensates chosen entities for political support.

Next, the money spills down into commercial banks and small businesses. They receive abundant free money and forgiven debt that gets repackaged as cheap mortgages, lines of credit, and grants.

Finally, a trickle of new money reaches its way to wage earners through stimulus checks or tax credits.

When the spout of new money closes, and the money attaches to investments or purchases, we end up with inflation. All of that fresh, easy money dilutes the existing old money.

The old money is earned from economic contributions. The new money is not. But since fiat is fungible, they are indistinguishable from each other. New and old money mixes, devaluing the old.

The funnel of new money didn't produce any goods or services. It just gave everyone more money, but disproportionately.

The top of the funnel will buy real estate, stocks, artwork, and other accredited, privileged, or higher net-worth assets. It drives up their prices. Now the economy looks good.

The media reports that the stock market is up, housing is up, and the economy is booming. They're not wrong. But they're not right.

The price increases do not correlate with economic output. There's simply a higher number on a price tag. Nothing else changes.

The bottom of the funnel receiving a $200 check discovers that their purchasing power requires $200 more to receive consumables like eggs or gasoline. And if they were saving for things like a house, they are further away from that dream by a wide margin. That dream house isn't only $200 more. It's $100,000 more due to the disproportionate distribution.

The top of the funnel's money drives big assets up, which pulls up the pricing for everything underneath those assets.

Real estate pricing alone will raise the prices of brokers, realtors, builders, contractors, materials, labor, trucks, designers, landscapers, appliances, furniture, delivery services, improvement stores, property taxes, and on and on and on.

As these services and wages increase, individuals buy more goods and services. When that demand increases, prices increase. When prices increase, consumers demand higher salaries from their employers. When employers have to pay higher wages, they sell their goods and services for more money. And the cycle continues.

All from one pour of money which came from the click of a computer key.

The Fed can print as much as it wants. It knows the cost is inflation. It knows it debases the value of all its fiat holders. But it has to fund the government's debt to fund its wars to enforce the fiat that pays its debt. It's a vicious cycle all in the name of fiat.

Wars, politics, and economics have "officially" collapsed civilizations. But all those were precipitated by the manipulation of their monetary system.

Citizens understand this. It's why we always seek better money. We always seek qualities that improve money to bring it closer to what it should and shouldn't be.

Throughout history, we have sought hard money. "Hard" money is difficult to censor, manipulate, obtain, seize, counterfeit, produce more of, or devalue.

We got close. We mined gold. We defined it as money. But now that we are off the gold standard, we never go back. The addiction to the money printer is too strong.

It is why money is broken. And it is why Bitcoin has surfaced as the remedy to this ailment.

Furs, feathers, fabrics, salt, stones, and wampum shells are just a few of the commodities that have been used as money for thousands of years. Due to supply manipulation (inflation), they all met the same demise. Each time, however, we learn something new about how to find and recognize better money.

At one point, salt was money. It was both currency and a store of value in Greece and Rome. In fact, the word "salary" derives from "salt," as Roman soldiers were paid in salt.

Some regimes and empires tried to limit who could make salt. But it was too plentiful and difficult to discern from an authorized salt maker or a peasant evaporating collected water from the sea.

Although light, portable, and decentralized, salt was somewhat easy to make. Why fight for the Roman army and risk your life in a barbaric war if you can boil sea water and produce salt crystals in the safety of your home?

Salt had other problems as a chosen money. It preserves food, is an integral part of a diet, and heals wounds. Because salt has utility outside of money, it degrades its value as money.

Money's only purpose should be money so that it works as an exchange token and nothing else.

When salt's market price was high, people limited its use as a commodity. They removed it from their diets and let their wounds infect. And since salt was procured relatively easily, they'd give up whatever specialized skill they possessed to create more salt.

You end up with an economy that values the money token itself and nothing else.

It's similar to the myth of Narcissus. He sees his reflection in a lake and is struck by how beautiful he is. He values his image so much that he can't do anything else. He eventually dies staring at himself.

If an economy only makes money, no new goods or services correlate to that new money. So the already existing, limited goods raise prices to match the higher quantity of money in the system.

Hard, sound money must enter an economy because it ties to productivity output. This is how a natural, healthy economy grows.

You work, provide value, are compensated, and spend. Your money is attached to your past work. Money without proof of work is counterfeit money.

Salt has some good qualities as money. Like gold or Bitcoin, salt requires work to introduce into the supply. Salt is also portable for small purchases.

It is divisible down to a single grain. And it is recognizable and verifiable by everyone. One only needs to taste a grain to confirm it's salt.

But salt isn't secure or durable. Others might notice if you store a large sack of salt in the corner of your home or drag it across town for a large purchase. And since salt dissolves within minutes once wet, imagine a rainstorm or spilled pot of water washing away your entire net worth.

And then there's censorship. Authorities eventually made it illegal for citizens to make salt. They only allowed a select few at the top to make it, including themselves. Sound familiar?

As a result of censorship, the decentralized money system for salt was replaced with a centralized one, debasing its value. When salt's value as money became worthless, it served its original purpose again, so it probably sits on your kitchen table rather than in a safe.

Another infamous form of money was the Aggry glass beads West Africans used for generations. People wore them as necklaces to move around the vast plains while hunting or farming.

Due to a lack of technology, the glass-making process took a lot of work and effort. There were intricate colors and patterns. As a result, beads were in short supply and had a low issuance rate into the bead supply. It made the beads hard and sound money for centuries.

The rate that newer money enters the existing supply of money is referred to as stock-to-flow.

Stock is the current supply of money.

Flow is the newly created money that adds to and increases the current supply.

In Africa's case, the stock was the total amount of glass beads all the Africans had in their economy at any one time. Flow was the newly "minted" influx of beads that joined the existing supply once they were created and spent into the economy. Those additional beads flowed into the current stock.

Stock-to-flow is an essential criterion for money to resist hyperinflation and succeed. Hard money needs as high a stock-to-flow as possible. You want the stock to be high compared to a much lower flow.

A low, predictable flow schedule can build a healthy money supply with natural market forces when rulers don't manipulate it. Gold has been an excellent example of this in the past. Bitcoin is now the perfect example of this in the present.

Based on the difficulty and expense of mining gold, the average rate at which anyone can bring new gold into the supply is low (around 2% per year). It makes its stock-to-flow high - high stock of existing gold and low flow of new gold.

Furthermore, because no one authority is responsible for introducing gold into the world, participation is open to all and pseudo-decentralized, aside from governmental regulations.

Anyone can grab a pick, an ax, and a pan and head into the mountains to mine gold. It requires proof of work. If you're willing to do that work, you deserve some gold.

But unlike salt, the work required to mine gold is monumentally more difficult. This retains gold's economic principle. It reduces the incentive to mine gold over anything else. If you can do anything else or have any skill, you would do that before trying to mine gold for a living.

Days of panning for gold are primarily obsolete and relegated to novelty. Over time, hard money increases its difficulty to obtain, and more energy is necessary. Gold closest to the surface has already been taken. One must go deeper to find more, which requires immense expense and permission.

Increased difficulty is a necessary component of proof of work systems. It helps secure and protect the integrity of the output of that work. In money's case, it shields against manipulation, inflation, and theft.

Bitcoin has the highest stock-to-flow of any money system there's ever been. Its issuance schedule is programmed and deterministic. There's no guesswork.

At the time of publication, 19.3 million Bitcoin have already been mined and are in the circulating supply. That's 92% of the entire Bitcoin that will ever be available.

It took only 14 years to reach this level. Yet it will take 117 years to finalize the remaining 8% of the total supply. The stock-to-flow rises as the new Bitcoin flow tightens and tightens.

In contrast, fiat has the lowest stock-to-flow of any money that has ever existed. After Covid hit, for example, the amount of new U.S. dollars created was 42% of the entire money supply. It rendered the existing fiat stock insanely low compared to the unfathomably high inflow of new money.

Two years later, prices on almost everything were roughly 42% higher on goods, services, and commodities. More money + the same amount of goods = higher prices on those goods. Very few products arrived post covid. The most extensive "product" was money itself.

Remember, this is dangerous whenever money incentivizes the creation of itself over other productivity. It will begin to enslave the holders of that money.

Globally the world printed somewhere around $17 trillion post-C-19. All of that gets repaid in the form of a deep recession, bear market, faltering real estate, inflation, debasement of currency, and overall wealth and time theft.

The zero cost of printing outsources to the high cost of human flourishing. It is devastating to an economy and its people.

The African Aggry beads had a solid, high stock-to-flow ratio. It was hard money in this sense. Beads were difficult and time-consuming to make, so those who chose to make them had to exert energy, learn, practice, buy materials, and perfect their skill to bring them into the system.

This proof of work was evident in the high value the glass beads carried. Most regular tribes wouldn't attempt to make more glass beads because it was more difficult than contributing to the economy with their personally acquired skills. It fosters economic coordination and growth when everyone performs at their peak in their area of expertise.

African beads were passed down over generations and used as dowries or heirlooms. It was money that could transcend time.

But that changed after European explorers visited the west coast of Africa. The travelers were surprised at how much the Africans valued these glass beads as a form of money. They especially found it odd since they could easily make these types of beads back home in Europe.

European businessmen realized they could take advantage of the African economy to benefit themselves.

Glass-making technology was much more advanced and ubiquitous in the Netherlands, Italy, and France. Thus if the African people were willing to do almost anything for more glass beads, there was a lopsided opportunity available to the importers.

The Europeans began an operation of shipping over the Aggry glass beads by the boatload. They could buy any product and command any service. Labor was as inexpensive as the plentiful beads that could stuff and sail over on ships.

As more beads entered the supply, each bead was worth less. Thus every trade required more beads. This challenged the African continent's economy as they watched everything priced in beads inflate.

But whereas the Africans mostly had to work for and earn the beads, the Europeans could make them at little cost. As with any money system, this imbalance permanently corrupts the system and enslaves those working for the money.

Eventually, the Africans became deeply indebted due to the beads' hyperinflation. Their family's life savings stored in beads eviscerated. Since there was no shortage of new beads, the original beads they had been saving for years as a symbol of their life's work could no longer retain their value.

Thus the Africans went into debt and had to borrow to make ends meet. They had no choice but to pay off their expenses by selling their labor to creditors (the Europeans).

This process facilitated the transatlantic slave trade. Europeans would sail over with ships loaded with glass beads and return home with Africans who owed them their labor for requiring more beads just to live.

Families even sold their own relatives. And to acquire more beads, kings and the wealthy elite sold off members of lower social classes. They needed as many beads as possible to protect themselves from becoming slaves.

This became one of the earliest known counterfeiting schemes of money.

But the Africans didn't give up easily. They discovered that they could create a different kind of glass bead. Perhaps it contained more coral or clay. It might have been more blueish. Regardless of the tactic, they started a sub-economy to give their indigenous glass beads more value than the counterfeit ones imported by the explorers.

The explorers would soon adapt and match the alternate-style beads. A game of cat-and-mouse persisted over the years. It deemed Africa's money unreliable and non-fungible. They could no longer trust or cooperate in trade when they had to verify which beads had value and which didn't.

Those left choosing the wrong color or style of beads for savings ended up enslaving themselves, quite literally.

The hyperinflation of glass beads caused the entire economy to trade away its wealth to the point it no longer had sovereignty over its system. Citizens had given up every ounce of freedom to a trade gone wrong due to the chosen money vessel.

No trade is more important than the one we make against our future selves.

For Africans, the unfortunate choice of Aggry glass beads led to the theft of over 12 million lives in the form of slavery from 1500 to 1800. 2 million of those lives never survived the voyage back to Europe. Of the 10 million that made it, they forcefully gave up 5,000 hours a year for an average of 40 years.

That stolen time only compounded when children were born into a world of slavery the minute they could walk.

In the end, African beads were a colossal failure on many levels. It emphasizes the value of pure, hard money and the immeasurable cost of money that can be counterfeited.

Beads couldn't transcend space. It's space that ultimately doomed them. Explorers who could reach Africa disrupted any border protection the beads may have originally had.

Beads couldn't transcend fungibility. One bead did not possess the same value as another. No one could be trusted because quality level had become necessary to value wealth. There will always be a problem with trust-based money.

Beads couldn't transcend their original high stock-to-flow ratio. Unlimited new supplies turned this ratio upside down to a low stock-to-flow. A money supply must be absolute or at least confined to a predictable and knowable number.

Beads couldn't transcend durability. They were breakable. They may have had a stone-like quality, but bad actors could crush or smash them.

And since the Aggry glass beads were worn as necklaces, they were visible for thieves and thus couldn't transcend security. Gold never learned this lesson and has caused many to lose life and limb for flexing it. Money should never be a flex.

The debt of today is no different than this ancient monetary slavery.

Fiat's inflation depletes the wealth of its holders, driving many of them to sacrifice more time to survive. With enough debt or high enough prices, there is no freedom of time, as time becomes worthless.

Holders of inflated money have little choice but to do whatever is necessary to acquire larger and larger amounts of it to maintain their same level of consumption.

The enslavers of the past shifted from explorers and businessmen to central banks and politicians.

Thankfully, the chains of slavery are primarily absent in most parts of the world. But moral decay and social collapse are the same under a corrupt monetary system.

7

PROOF OF VALUE

"I think there is a world market for maybe five computers."

Thomas Watson, chairman of IBM, 1943

P roponents of gold employ the wrong tactic when they argue why gold is better money than Bitcoin. They often highlight that gold has intrinsic value, but Bitcoin does not. They say that you can at least use gold in jewelry, microchips, and dentistry.

What can you use Bitcoin for? How do I touch it, hold it, or do anything with it? Bitcoin is just 1s and 0s.

Ironically, this argument only proves why Bitcoin is superior to gold as money.

The fallacy is to think that money needs to have intrinsic value. Any outside use for a money token only detracts and distorts what should otherwise be a pure and clear signal for monetary language.

People use gold as jewelry because it is money, not the other way around. Similar to Africa's glass beads, gold became jewelry as a way to transport it. You wouldn't leave valuables at home for fear of theft, so you'd fashion it into a necklace, bracelet, or belt to carry and keep safe.

As some gained excessive wealth with gold or glass beads, they flaunted it by placing necklaces on the outside of their clothing. The original intention was always to hide wealth, not showcase it. But money became a way to impress others. It was a flex.

Diamonds are also a popular piece of jewelry. They are just as big a flex, if not bigger, than gold. They are also just as difficult to mine and bring into the supply. It is why they, too, have been a past form of money.

But unlike gold and beads, diamonds aren't fungible, so they failed as money. No two diamonds are alike. There's no unit of account. Five 1 oz diamonds are not equal to a 5 oz diamond.

Jewelry won't fail without gold. Microchips won't fail without gold.

Cheaper metal substitutes like aluminum, copper, and silver are all used in today's microchips. And any dentist will tell you that you don't need metal in your mouth. It is an archaic and potentially unhealthy option now replaced with safer composites.

Nevertheless, gold is used in some medical and aerospace applications for its durability, electricity transmission, and ability to deflect corrosion. It's a versatile metal.

Even though there are substitutes for gold, it is valued for its inherent physical attributes aside from its value as money. Therefore gold has two pricing mechanisms at play, both as money and as a utility.

Goldbugs are correct: gold has intrinsic value. Like sheep, salt, oil, fabrics, cattle, hides, or tobacco, gold is a physical commodity that people can value outside of just money.

But valuing the physical usefulness of a commodity is not what makes that commodity money. It is unrelated.

The utility of these commodities essentially made them impure money, as displayed in the previous chapter. Salt has now returned to its utility, erasing its entire value as money.

The same goes for tobacco, used as money during colonial times until people smoked their wealth away. It partially died as money due to its intrinsic value.

Despite its intrinsic value, gold has survived and prospered as the best money for centuries. It proves how strong some of the other qualities of gold are that it has survived this long.

Still, the flawed thinking is that gold has value as money because it has intrinsic value.

Fiat has no intrinsic value whatsoever. This makes it a strong currency. Other than using it for trade, you can't use modern-day currency for any other purpose. You can't eat it, fuel your car, or water your lawn with it.

You can do nothing with fiat other than burn it to temporarily keep warm if you have the paper version. And in countries with severe hyperinflation, this is literally what they do, as it has more utility than value.

Fiat is just an exchange token, as it should be. Of course, fiat is terrible money for all of the obvious reasons, but as far as intrinsic value is concerned, it works because there is none.

The same goes for the Aggry glass beads. They worked in part because there was absolutely no intrinsic value. They served no purpose outside of a store of value and intermediary between two parties. No one could build houses with them, read books with them, or use them as medicine.

Africans could trust that they could store the beads with them and carry their value without rotting, decaying, or being accidentally used for another purpose, such as salt. You don't want your teenager waking up hungry at night and eating your family's wealth.

Language also has no intrinsic value, yet it is perhaps our most valuable tool. We can't see or touch language. But placed in the proper order, words transfer value back and forth on a language network.

Money is the language of trade.

We can communicate, exchange ideas, thoughts, education, direction, and coordinate our intentions with language. And like Bitcoin, language can be stored in our heads, carried anywhere in the world, and kept private.

Money must be valueless compared to the trade it is consummating, even if that trade is with our future self (store of value).

It is difficult for money to store information when there is inherent value, like a piece of wood, a computer, a horse, a bucket of water, or a vacuum cleaner. None of these have ever been successful forms of money. They have too much intrinsic value.

Money is a network technology. It is the agnostic referee that allows completely different sides to communicate.

Look at a telephone landline, email, or Facebook - language technologies. On their own, they have zero intrinsic value. If you are the only one with email, you can't do anything with it. If you are the only one on Facebook, it serves no purpose.

When landlines first surfaced, they weren't valuable if you were the only one on your block with a phone. Who could you call? When a neighbor finally got a phone, you suddenly went from one node to two nodes. You could call them, and they could call you. There were two possible transmission options.

When an additional two neighbors joined, there were four nodes. Due to network effects, doubling the number of nodes from two to four exponentially multiplies the transmission options. Just 4 nodes now give you 12 combinations of phone calls. And so on.

People observe others joining a network, which motivates them to join and participate with their peers or businesses. It's how payment networks like Venmo or PayPal rise in popularity. Those two serve no purpose if you are the only node on the network.

You can create your own language. Does it have value? Not if you're the only one who speaks it. But as others learn your language and join your network, it has immense value - ditto for the telephone, email, Facebook, and Bitcoin.

Money is this same network but for the value of past time brought forward in the future. And without intrinsic value, money can fractionalize and divide this value for present consumption. If money has intrinsic value, like cattle, that trade is influenced by what else the cattle can do.

If gold had zero utility, it wouldn't reduce its ability to be money. It would only harden its proposition as money. Gold would become better money without influence of its utility on electronics.

Goldbugs and critics are correct: Bitcoin has no intrinsic value at all.

Bitcoin can't be used for anything outside of money. It is perfect money because it was built to be... perfect money. It wasn't discovered or ever used as anything else. It was created to solve all of the flaws and limitations of prior money systems. And one of those is intrinsic value.

Mark Cuban once quipped that he'd rather have a banana than Bitcoin because at least he can eat a banana. But what he failed to understand is that you would never want to eat money.

Predictably, Cuban has since become a loud advocate in favor of Bitcoin, as have many initial shoot-from-the-hip critics who haven't yet learned about it.

Bitcoin can't be used for dental fillings, to cure meat, or to wear as jewelry. You can't smoke it or eat it. And there's no way to flaunt or flex it other than by telling someone how much you have (bad idea, by the way). Bitcoin is the first money not to have a single utilitarian purpose outside of money.

The purpose of Bitcoin is to protect wealth with decentralized cryptographic software and transact any portion of that wealth permissionlessly to anyone, anywhere, anytime, regardless of bias.

Bitcoin's promise is to allow anyone to acquire it at the same price as anyone else without any preference, state interference, or manipulation.

No one can unfairly make it, take it, or fake it. Only the holder of Bitcoin has full property rights to do whatever they want with it. There is no authority or law to tell someone to transact or save in Bitcoin.

Like gold, Bitcoin has become money by merit. It's chosen by the people, evidenced by the increasing number of users, wallets, and market cap over time. Although sentiment has dipped in correlation to Bitcoin's market price, adoption has not. It has only gone up and will continue to go up.

All the best monetary systems throughout history became so because the people chose it, not a government. If an authority has to force you to choose a form of money, there's probably something wrong with it.

Bitcoin may have no intrinsic value, but the Bitcoin network is filled with it. The network has immense utility. This is where you need tangible use in the piping and plumbing of the money infrastructure. You need it in the system with which the money moves and settles globally for everyone.

The Bitcoin network is a vast web of decentralized rails on which Bitcoin the token rolls from node to node (user to user). This network continues to replace the dated and slow traditional money rails that commerce is accustomed to.

Even for those who want nothing to do with Bitcoin the token, their currency of choice (dollars, yen, euros, etc.) can transact and settle on Bitcoin's network, as described earlier with Lightning. Any fiat currency can move to a more efficient and effective superhighway where intermediaries, permission, and fees disappear.

As people learn about Bitcoin, they eventually learn about the financial network.

It's like learning about Fedwire and Swift, which is the plumbing for USD. Although fiat is trending to zero due to inflation, its plumbing is not. It's instrumental. Bitcoin's plumbing, however, is far superior, more efficient, effective, and inclusive than Fedwire or Swift.

Not surprisingly, the continent of Africa currently has one of the fastest adoptions of Bitcoin in the world, in large part due to the Bitcoin network. Countries like Botswana, Kenya, Morocco, Nigeria, South Africa, and Zimbabwe depend on the Bitcoin network to circumvent monetary restrictions.

With the unfortunate aftermath of Aggry beads and the French colonialism that followed, Africa was left without any monetary sovereignty. Most of the 1.4 billion people are still unbanked or under predatory, fractured banking systems with high fees and censorship.

76% of Kenyans don't have any banking whatsoever. They're forced to use expensive payment systems equivalent to our pay-day loan and check-cashing services. It's no wonder they crave a fair and universal language for money.

Over 2,000 different languages exist in Africa across 54 countries. Even exchanging amongst their people is a monumental effort with varying currencies and regulations. But one language that unites everyone is math and value.

25 million Africans live outside of Africa. Their families back home depend on them to send them money to survive. But remittance payments have an average of 9% in fees due to predatory banking transfers and corrupt government restrictions.

Inflation in Zimbabwe alone reaches 200% in some years. Not 20%, 200%! Africans simply can't save or preserve any of their work with debasement like that. Now add 9% remittance fees to this.

Bitcoin reduces this friction to literal fractions of a penny and transfers within seconds rather than weeks, allowing families to retain their value outside any jurisdiction. It's estimated that at least 30% of Africa's citizens in more developed regions own and transact in Bitcoin.

Africans in remote places with no internet access use "feature phones," which can transact in Bitcoin with simple SMS (texting) from user to user.

Africa is just one example showing the Bitcoin network's utility value. Vietnam and the Philippines are two of the fastest adopters of Bitcoin's Lightning Network for payments. They, too, are debased at the state level conducting business in their currency. And getting money in or out of their country is difficult, if possible.

Bitcoin, the token, has immense incidental value because it is money. It has monetary value as a consequence of its hard money characteristics. It is an important distinction and partially the whole point of Bitcoin - for the people, by the people, the way a democracy promises to be but rarely is.

Money by merit results from scarcity, portability, durability, divisibility, and recognizability. The degree to which a commodity carries those qualities defines its hardness.

Then, to reach a level of purity, money needs to add to these qualities the ability to be trustless, transparent, unhackable, and censorship-resistant. Money can never hold these characteristics if any person, entity, or group controls it.

Bitcoin's value is in fulfilling the job requirements of hard money - to transfer and store value without fear of theft. Past money systems have failed for a lack of meeting these criteria.

8

PROOF OF WORK

"The U.S. Navy is not going to be caught napping."

Secretary of the U.S. Navy, Frank Knox, Dec 4, 1941 (3 days
before the attack on Pearl Harbor)

One form of money I call "Flintstones Bitcoin" came surprisingly close to becoming "Bitcoin" in the 1800s. In what is now Micronesia, the islands of Yap made rai stones their form of money.

These were different from the type of stones you skip across a lake. These were gigantic slabs of limestone as big as 8 to 12 feet high and too heavy to move anywhere. Many were as big as the huts people lived in, requiring up to 20 men to move.

The island of Yap itself didn't naturally possess limestone. To add a single rai stone to the economy required a risky endeavor of dozens of men on rafts and canoes. They would sail the high seas over 250 miles away to the island of Palau.

After months of labor on Palau, men quarried the limestone into a sizeable donut-shaped monolith (almost like the largest "coin" you've ever seen) and onto the rafts to trek back to Yap. Men died during this voyage, attempting to navigate a massive rock across the ocean.

Once back home on the island of Yap with the new rai stone, the lead voyager of the expedition would announce to the village that this was his stone. He rewarded the workers who survived by assigning them fractions of the rock. The rest was his to eventually spend into Yap's economy.

Due to the weight and sheer size of the rai stone, the owner could place it anywhere on the island, out in the open, for everyone to see. It just sat there like a statue. There was no need to hide or keep it on your land. They were too heavy for anyone to move or take without everyone noticing. It would be the first of many qualities that made the stones hard money.

When the rock owner needed to buy goods or services, he marked it on the rock's face, announcing it to the village. The rock became an open and auditable ledger, like a giant chalkboard. There was no dispute about who had portions of value from each stone on the island.

Rather than haul salt around on your back or donkey, one would "move" money by announcement.

"Joe gives 4 units to Lisa" gets recorded on the 10,000-unit rock. Then when Lisa wants to spend those 4 units, she, in turn, announces that those 4 units go to Jeremy. And so on. The whole island can confirm this. No quarrels. No guessing.

The rai stone wasn't physically portable but was virtually portable. It wasn't physically divisible but was virtually divisible - no need to break up or destroy the rock. And it was indestructible. It could withstand any weather or theft due to its size and weight.

Because the rai stone was cumbersome and life-threatening to "mint," it had a high stock-to-flow ratio and built-in fungibility. The existing stock of rocks was visible to all. The flow of new stones into the supply was excruciatingly slow (thus low) due to the difficulty of its proof of work.

No one valued one rock more than the next, as they all carried the same glistening limestone from the island of Palau. The size only varied the quantity of value, not the quality.

The rai stone had zero intrinsic value. It served no purpose beyond storing and transferring value to the Yapese people. Maybe kids climbed on them or someone would use it to get a better view of the water. But no one valued the rock for this activity. It was solely to store and transact one's wealth.

Fiat requires one to trust a government, trust a money supply, trust a money wire, trust a transaction, and trust a bank. The rai stone didn't have these issues because the islanders didn't have to trust anyone.

That was the key. It wasn't about finding someone you could trust. It was about finding a way not to have to trust. The rai stone found a trustless money system 200 years before Bitcoin.

This trustless way of viewing money hadn't existed before.

No one could fake getting a 6-ton rock onto an island with exhausted and hungry men from a 3-month expedition of quarrying and then sailing 500 miles round trip. And there was no need for intermediaries to reduce value or forbid a transaction. It was permissionless.

The leaders of Yap couldn't make a rock appear and inflate the economy. Equal to citizens, leaders would have to command a group of strong, adventurous men to expend energy and wrestle a big rock. It required proof of work, just like mining gold or mining Bitcoin. This made it decentralized.

Proof of work is so valuable when it comes to money that you don't even have to see the money. Remember, this is a common critique related to intrinsic value.

Where is it? How do I hold it? How can I see it? We are accustomed to tangible currencies, commodities, and property. Most things we invest in have physicality.

The internet is a language and network technology. Rather than English or German, its language is code. You can't touch the internet. It's invisible. But who wouldn't want to invest in the internet if they could go back in time and if it was an investable asset?

How can anything of value be intangible? Ask the 2.4 billion Christians in the world or the 6 billion religious people who place importance on something they can't see or touch.

Bitcoin supersedes the value of language or religion by transcending censorship.

Language and religion have imprisoned and silenced many journalists, advocates, believers, and thinkers throughout history. Because Bitcoin is apolitical and only adheres to the laws of math, it can't upset anyone at someone else's expense.

Bitcoin is legally defined and protected in the U.S. Code as free speech. But this makes no difference for countries who want to ban it.

Even so, no country has ever successfully banned the internet. China, Cuba, Iran, Turkey, Saudi Arabia, etc., all find a way to use the internet at times when it's banned or curtailed. You can't stop people and their will.

Over 200 years ago, the Yapese understood that value transcends physicality. They understood the importance of proof of work so much that they eventually placed value on invisibility.

A group of men once returned to the island of Palau with another large rai stone ready to enter into the Yapese money supply. But they couldn't get to Yap's shore due to severe storms in the bay. They had to anchor and wait until they could safely navigate onto land.

After days of battling the weather, the stormy seas capsized the rafts, and the huge rai stone sank to the bay's bottom.

When the men eventually reached Yap's shore with their tattered rafts and canoes, the village accepted the value of the underwater rock as if it were sitting right there on the island alongside the others.

The community decided that an invisible rock was no less valuable than a visible one because there was proof of work.

The group of men had no reason to lie. They were absent for months, bruised, some dead. They proved their work. And so the rock became part of the economy and remained so for generations. It was, in some sense, the first form of virtual money, like Bitcoin.

Like the rai stone, Bitcoin doesn't technically move anywhere. It just sits there for everyone to verify. We use helpful analogies when we say "send," "receive," or "wallet."

We transfer access on the Bitcoin network, just like the rai stone. We transfer ownership of that access from one person to another.

If you own Bitcoin, you own the secret keys that access the location of that Bitcoin. You can transfer value over to someone else so that they can access that Bitcoin with their secret keys.

Bitcoin miners bring Bitcoin from the total programmed supply into the circulating supply. They must attach their computers to electricity to compute numbers.

Bitcoin miners prove their work when they combine transactions from senders and receivers into a long list (a block). Finally, they broadcast this block of transactions to everyone on the network, just like the Yapese announce and scribble on their stone.

Because miners have to pay for the costs of computers and electricity, once they mine some Bitcoin, they sell it into the Bitcoin economy to compensate for their work. This Bitcoin distributes via exchanges to non-miners who then save or transact in it.

The same goes for the Yapese. The value of the rai stone weaves its way into the Yap economy when the owners spend off portions to cover their costs. Everyone in the economy can act as a "node" - a part of the network.

Each node can equally see and validate transactions on the rock. When hundreds of Yapese see the writing on a stone, it takes just one of them to raise their hand and say, "Whoa, that transaction is incorrect. Jill doesn't have 5 pebbles to send to Jeff. She only has 2 pebbles. Deny!" And so the transaction is null and void.

Anyone on the Bitcoin network can be a node when they download the free software onto their computer. They can view all of the transactions in the past and present. They then verify and validate whether a transaction is true or false.

When nodes from all over the world, who don't know each other, unanimously say a transaction is valid, it goes through and becomes cemented in Bitcoin's blockchain.

Bitcoin can be thought of as a modern-day, abstract accounting system that digitizes what the rai stones accomplished in their antiquated way. Both money systems remove the problem of physicality because access to ownership transfers rather than any tangible item.

With Bitcoin, no one must carry, wear, or transport something across town. All 21 million Bitcoin are around us, connected via all its users (nodes) in almost every country.

But because Bitcoin didn't exist for the Yapese people, eventually, the rai stone proved to have a flaw in its system. Like the Aggry beads, it couldn't resist interference and manipulation.

An Irishman discovered the Yapese and their peculiar rock donut economy. He calculated that he could be the wealthiest man on the island with his larger, faster ships and superior quarry technology back home. So he sailed to Palau, quarried the limestone, and brought it to the island where he could command any services.

The Yapese respected the Irishman. There was proof of his work. But the problem was the drastic surge in stock-to-flow. Suddenly the low, recognizable flow of new money into the economy turned into a waterfall of new money.

Inflation was high since the Irishman inundated the island with rai stones. It is no different than a central bank injecting more money into its fiat supply.

Germans later arrived and trumped the Irishman's manipulation. They took over governance and outlawed the Yapese from sailing more than 200 miles. It prevented them from traveling the 250-mile distance to the island of Palau to quarry rai stones.

As an authority backed by force, the Germans removed the decentralized nature of the rai stones and replaced it with their centralized control. The Germans were permitted to sail and grab all the rai stones they wanted to benefit their own spending. But the Yapese couldn't.

By definition, rai stones became fiat. They were no longer money and were on a high inflation trend.

Like Africans, the Yapese tried to prevent this money manipulation. They attempted to assign value to older stones to separate those considered counterfeit from intruders.

But this non-fungibility and inflation squeezed out every ounce of value the people had. They became slaves to their debt as new arrivals with big rai stones could own anything and, unfortunately, anyone.

Societies always devolve into wealth debasement and slavery when only a privileged few can create money. History shows us that this exploitation leads to the collapse of civilizations.

Money creation, if possible, is too tempting to resist. So it can never be possible in the first place for it to be pure money.

The printing of fiat is no different than Africa's Aggry beads or Yap's rai stones. It steals people's life force.

The U.S. government has stolen an average of about 7.5% from its citizens every year since 1980. If the average wage-earner works 40 hours a week or 2,000 hours per year, that's equivalent to enslaving almost 12 million people over 40 years. This usurps the enslavement of the trans-Atlantic slave trade in wealth terms by about 350% per year for each of those 40 years.

And the U.S. is the least bad by orders of magnitude compared to the other 190 countries, who are all inflating much worse than we are.

Because the world is now digitally connected, we see the failures of imperfect money and the desperate need for perfect money.

Bitcoin is on a path to becoming the most salable money we've ever had. It is the first financial asset (Bitcoin the token) and economic infrastructure (Bitcoin the network) all rolled into one (simply Bitcoin).

Bitcoin is complete sovereignty for anyone. Anyone can make this choice regardless of any authority or jurisdiction. It is the first independent property that can't be taken away or cheated. It is impervious to invaders, hackers, or governments.

Anything that can be taken from you was never yours to begin with. And if it's in someone else's custody, it's not yours.

If an entity can place a lien on it, it's not yours. If it can be diluted or altered, it's not yours. If an entity that administers it can go under, it's not yours. If it can default, it's not yours. If a bank can freeze it, it's not yours. Even cash is just a rented coupon that can be recalled anytime.

In many ways, Bitcoin is the first actual property ever unequivocally and immutably ours. It's "ours" in that it is wholly yours but also wholly mine and anyone else's who wants it. But because it's digital and decentralized, no one can touch it.

Bitcoin lives everywhere at once. This concept is difficult for Luddites. It lives on everyone else's ledger, but no one can manipulate it.

For the wealthy, Bitcoin is a pile of billions of dollars of cash and the Hope Diamond encased in bullet-proof glass inside Fort Knox with millions of armed guards. And for the poor, Bitcoin is freedom, access, and opportunity.

Only you have control of Bitcoin (when you hold your own secret keys). That's what money is supposed to be. Money is supposed to accurately and holistically capture and compress your life energy into a tradable token.

Bitcoin is a promise that because of your contribution to society and your intellectual or physical exertion of energy, it is yours to keep or spend as you see fit.

Bitcoin embraces the transformation of resources with incorruptibility. There is no risk of seizure or censorship based on the work done. Once we've proved our work, we can secure it forever with Bitcoin.

9
PROOF OF CUSTODY

"If excessive smoking actually plays a role in the production of lung cancer, it seems to be a minor one."

W.C. Hueper, National Cancer Institute, 1954

E ven though President Roosevelt legally banned gold in 1933, the government didn't go knocking door to door at citizens' homes asking to see what was under their floorboards or hidden in a wall.

Mostly, those who held gold with a custodian, such as a bank, had to relinquish their gold. Gold advocates highlight this as a justification for self-custody rather than with an institution. When you have it, you own it. When you don't have it, you don't.

Part of the responsibility of having full property rights and sovereignty is being accountable for that property.

Storing what is meant to be 100% yours with a third party somewhat defeats the purpose, as it isn't technically or legally yours. A user must trust that a custodian will someday give them the exact value claimed on a statement balance.

Gold's analog nature limits its use as money if held in self-custody buried in a backyard with an "X" mark. Even in a safe or basement, how difficult is it to partition that gold for services or quickly sell it in an emergency?

And how do you flee with gold in a hurry, hide it, transport it, and then prove to someone else that it's real? How do you avoid someone stealing it from you during this process?

Exchanges, ETFs, and mutual funds make buying and selling gold easy and convenient. But no physical gold changes hands.

Ironically, gold set out to solve the manipulation and permission of the state with scarcity and sovereignty, when most who "hold" gold do so via a custodian that is permissioned by the state.

ETFs and exchanges give users paper gold. The company may physically own gold as regulators require, but that doesn't mean it's a user's gold. And it doesn't mean they don't rehypothecate it, as is standard banking procedure.

There is over $240 trillion in paper gold, yet only $12 trillion of actual, physical gold. It is rehypothecated at 20 to 1! It takes us back to when the Nixon Administration printed fiat in 1971, inflating the world's money.

How can gold be an escape from fiat inflation if the majority of gold held is just printable paper? Isn't this the same problem all over again?

Paper gold solves the archaic custody issue of having to strong-arm your wealth like Fort Knox. But it brings back the same problems gold proponents fight to solve.

Investors want to avoid the impracticality of gold self-custody. But this comes at the expense of "printing" gold. With paper, the supply is unlimited. Now you've taken one of the oldest and hardest forms of money and made it soft, just like fiat.

It is one of the reasons gold's value has barely budged for over 4 decades. When paper claims can be created and traded without actual gold having to settle between buyers and sellers, it violates the principles of demand and supply that set market prices.

A gold exchange can give you as much gold as you want at whatever price they set if they don't have to settle actual gold. And the same goes for when you sell.

As long as there isn't a bank run on actual gold, the gold market is really one of paper. The real gold market becomes a second layer of gold, more like a currency than money.

Gold may have as much as 1 billion holders or 12.5% of the world's population. Places like India and Saudi Arabia have the highest concentration of goldbugs, whereas, in the U.S., about 10% of the population holds gold.

But most of this comes from older generations, before the digitization of our modern world. And most of this is now on an exchange like a retirement account or hedge fund.

Younger generations find gold way too cumbersome and analog. The percentage of millennials who own gold is under 5%. And most of that is due to inheritance or gifting, including jewelry. It's rare to find a millennial who purposefully buys physical gold.

Less than 1% of Gen Z owns gold. Again, most of this is due to gifts from boomer grandparents. The first choice of savings for Gen Z is Bitcoin. And it's been called "the millennial savings account" by numerous millennial journalists. Here in the U.S., over 30% of millennials own Bitcoin.

If you add up the value of all gold held by everyone in the world, priced in today's dollars, you will arrive at just over $12 trillion. That's gold's market capitalization. It is roughly 30 times that of Bitcoin's market cap at the time of publication.

As Bitcoin continues to climb through its early adoption phase, its market cap will fluctuate wildly with the price. In November 2021, when Bitcoin was at $69,000, its market cap was almost $1.3 trillion. Give Bitcoin another decade; it may swallow most of gold's market cap.

Remember, Bitcoin can be viewed as digital gold. It is better gold than gold.

If the only future adopters of Bitcoin were those shifting from gold, then Bitcoin's price would shoot into the multiple million USD per single Bitcoin. This is just from some of the gold owners switching over to Bitcoin to eliminate gold's limitations in the modern world.

In all fairness, Bitcoin will experience some of the same paper inflation as gold. Exchanges and financial companies can set up whatever business they want, like a gold dealer or gold exchange. Third parties can rehypothecate Bitcoin.

Financial companies can lend Bitcoin out, leverage it, and tell you they're holding your Bitcoin when, in fact, they're not. They may take your deposit of 5 Bitcoin but lend all of it out to someone else, essentially doubling the amount of Bitcoin in paper terms to 10 Bitcoin.

We saw this rehypothecation during the custody collapse of 2022. The implosion of CeFi (Centralized Finance) crypto companies brought Bitcoin's price down from its highs of $69k to $15k. Companies like Celsisus, Voyager, BlockFi, and FTX filed bankruptcy when they lent out more crypto than they actually had.

Unlike traditional finance banks, crypto lenders aren't FDIC insured, at least for crypto balances. These companies aren't banks, aren't regulated, and are largely off-shore.

Bitcoin is, of course, separate and unrelated to crypto. Bitcoin is regulated and legally defined as a commodity. But this doesn't stop companies, whether intentions are good or bad, from rehypothecation.

Full disclosure: Yours truly was also caught up in the custody collapse. In sum, these exchanges offered attractive rates for storing Bitcoin (and crypto) on their exchanges. They offered anywhere from 5 to 10%.

These exchanges sold themselves as safe havens to store your Bitcoin. Why mess with clunky hardware wallets you might lose or forget a password to? And while you're at it, why not earn interest by locking it up? It was an enticing sales pitch.

With users' deposits, whether Bitcoin or crypto, including even USD, the exchanges lent it out at higher rates to risky hedge funds such as Three Arrows Capital (3AC). 3AC, in turn, staked much of their borrowed funds on a Ponzi platform promising 20%+ returns.

Once the music stopped, 3AC defaulted on its loans, and all the big exchanges were left with huge holes in their balance sheets. They didn't have the Bitcoin or crypto that their users' account balances displayed. But like a typical Ponzi, they allowed initial users to withdraw funds saying everything was fine.

Celsius said everything was fine. No need to panic. Voyager said everything was fine. No need to panic. BlockFi said everything was fine. No need to panic. FTX said everything was fine. No need to panic.

In each case, there was a need to panic.

FTX had been selling paper Bitcoin and, in some cases, to these other exchanges. FTX was the exchange of exchanges since they had so much money. But, of course, they didn't.

By the time FTX filed bankruptcy, they had owned less than 1 Bitcoin on their exchange. This created two problems.

First, it prevented Bitcoin from reaching its natural market price - scarcity was removed. Bitcoin was headed straight to $100k in late 2021 but precipitously fell after reaching $69k when exchange misconduct first surfaced.

Like paper gold, there are no accurate price signals if a Bitcoin exchange can sell fake Bitcoin at whatever price they set.

Lending out a small percentage of your Bitcoin with proper risk controls can work. It is a standard business model that has served people and businesses since banking began. That's all a savings account is - lending your money to the bank.

But a surging Bitcoin market blinded many new companies to counterparty risk when they began lending without collateral. They hoped Bitcoin's market price would only climb, in which case they could cover their customers' deposits.

Second, the revelation of this risk caused many newcomers to lose trust. Apparently, all of the critics were right. Bitcoin was one big Ponzi scheme.

But anyone who held Bitcoin in their own custody still has that Bitcoin today. Nothing has changed except short-term price signals, which ebb and flow in 4-year cycles anyway.

When you self-custody Bitcoin, it is like having the digital version of tangible gold in your safe. But this safe isn't at home, the bank, or the cloud. It is everywhere, on every other user's computer, all at once. But it can only be accessed by you if it is your Bitcoin.

In hindsight, this was bound to happen, and healthy that it happened. It was one big reminder of some of the tenets behind Bitcoin's value proposition. And one of them is self-custody.

Bitcoin's design solves money printing and manipulation. But when held on an exchange, it gives that business free reign to do whatever they want with your Bitcoin.

In FTX's case, they never gave you Bitcoin. They gave you a number on a screen. FTX and the others looked slick. They had user-friendly interfaces and used words like "trust," "secure," and "safe."

Bitcoin's security, safety, and trust are already built into its protocol. No third party is needed, although one may be desired.

There are a lot of reputable exchanges that don't rehypothecate your Bitcoin.

Places like Swan Bitcoin, River Financial, or Unchained Capital have automatic features where you buy Bitcoin and transfer straight to your cold, offline wallet. They even encourage you to get it off their platform right after you buy. And none of these companies allow you to purchase or transact in any crypto. Bitcoin only.

Anyone can always buy Bitcoin on Robinhood, Coinbase, Cashapp, or one of the other hundred existing apps. It makes no difference. What's important is that you *immediately* send that Bitcoin back to your own wallet, not the exchange's wallet.

Every time buyers take possession of their Bitcoin, they secure the scarcity of Bitcoin's total circulating supply. This keeps the exchanges in line with Bitcoin's price where it should be, reflecting its superior monetary properties.

With so many wallets and options to hold your own Bitcoin, which ones do you choose?

What mostly matters is that you hold the 12 or 24 seed words that create and keep your secret keys. That is of utmost importance. Everything else is bells and whistles.

Ideally, you want a wallet that is completely detached from the internet so no online hacker has a chance to reach it, even if they could.

Hardware wallets like ColdCard, Ledger, Trezor, Seedsigner, or Bitbox hold your secret keys offline in your own physical device. You (and only you) separately hold your seed words as backups to recreate this wallet should you lose it.

With this self-custody setup, you are the bank. You control 100% of your Bitcoin. You can clone your hardware wallet as often as possible since you have the original seed words. Thus, you are the bank, but with the benefit of having as many branches of that bank as you find necessary.

It doesn't matter which Chase bank I enter, anywhere in the country. I can equally access and transact with USD. The same goes for Bitcoin wallets that are created with seed words.

Mobile wallets like Muun or BlueWallet have the convenience of living on your phone rather than a hardware wallet. They, too, utilize your seed words to create the secret keys. It's your Bitcoin.

Phone wallets are great for smaller transactions. There are hundreds of them available. But they are technically less secure because they are connected to the internet.

For long-term wealth, always use a hardware wallet. I like to think of a hardware wallet as my savings account and a mobile wallet as my checking account.

Beyond that, multi-signature options might be the best option for most. It is what I personally use to keep myself from making a mistake and prevent bad actors from having any single point of access to my Bitcoin.

I could be attacked at gunpoint in my own house, and a criminal would not be able to acquire my Bitcoin due to my multi-signature setup. Even I can't access it without specific steps that would expose anyone else if I were under duress.

Most Bitcoin holders store each of their multi-signature signing devices in different geographical locations. Some might be in a bank vault, some with a trust attorney, and some with other family members in a different state.

The security options are almost endless in how, where, and what configuration you can use to store the keys to your Bitcoin. These are the creative decisions one is afforded with sovereignty.

Bitcoin might be one of the most challenging assets to steal. Unlike stealing a bike or snatching 200 bucks out of a wallet, Bitcoin is entirely trackable and traceable. Depending on the amount stolen, the FBI gets involved and follows the money.

This is not to say one should be lazy with their security or flaunt their Bitcoin. It's to say that one shouldn't avoid Bitcoin because they think it'll attract criminals. There are much easier ways for criminals to steal value from someone than a transparent and open ledger that leads to every wallet and exchange.

Companies like Unchained Capital or Casa Hodl (not a misspelling) help you with multi-signature setups. This means that rather than one set of 12 or 24 seed words, you have several sets necessary to generate your secret keys.

For example, the most popular multi-signature setup is 2 of 3. This means you have 3 sets of keys. At least 2 of those 3 sets are needed to access your Bitcoin.

Multi-signature works great for legacy solutions where you keep 1 key, 1 key is given to a trustee or family member, and 1 key is stored with

Unchained or Casa. Since 2 keys are necessary, Unchained or Casa are optional to transact. All you need is you and your trustee.

But should you pass, your setup will allow your trustee to contact Unchained or Casa with proof of your death, and access your Bitcoin with the 2 surviving keys.

Greater numbers of keys aren't necessary for individuals. But sometimes partnerships, institutions, or corporations use a 5 of 9 setup. It is helpful so no rogue individual can steal the company's funds. Moving the company's Bitcoin balance takes at least 5 of the 9 board members.

Any configuration is possible. 2 of 2, 3 of 5, 8 of 15, etc. You can select the option that fits your situation. For most, just having 1 private set of keys is all that is necessary. This is technically a 1 of 1 setup.

Again, as I can't emphasize this enough, it's important that you have keys in the first place. Beyond that, it's optimization and customization for your situation.

Once you have your own seed words, you can copy them, hide them, split them up, engrave them in steel, and even geographically separate them. You can get creative in where or how you access them, including memorizing them as part of a poem or song.

You want to think through backup options on top of backup options in case your house burns down or your Aunt Edna loses the backup you had her hold for you.

I know it seems like Bitcoiners are preppers who hide a cache of guns in bomb silos and think the end of the world is coming. But most are bright economists, investors, engineers, accountants, philosophers, innovators, historians, mathematicians, environmentalists, software developers, gamers, and critical thinkers.

Add whatever you do to this list, as Bitcoin is for everyone.

Bitcoin's custody and wallets are vastly improving day by day. We are still at the dial-up phase of the internet, where simply logging on is clunky. By the time you read or listen to this book, there might be easier solutions.

Bitcoiners from prior bull/bear cycles have learned the lessons of self-custody. Every 4 years, we continue to witness new products and services, some of which unfortunately arrive from bad actors.

4 years before the CeFi scams were the ICO scams. These Initial Coin Offerings allowed anyone to invest in new altcoins before they hit the market. Since most people are cut off from investing in stock market IPOs, ICOs became highly attractive in 2018. But as many altcoins eventually do, they fell to their market value of $0.

The ICO scams pulled Bitcoin's price down from $20,000 to $3,200, an 84% drop. By comparison, the CeFi scams of 2022 dropped Bitcoin from $69,400 to $15,500, a 77% drop. And like clockwork, the bears before that went from $1,000 to $200, an 80% drop, and before that, from $32 to $0.01, a 99% drop!

Every single time the cause was a third party trying to monetize and leverage on top of Bitcoin or crypto. Each time, the market gets greedy and confident. And every time there's a shakeout of poor decisions, mismanaged exchanges, and a slow crawl from crypto back to the only fully self-sovereign asset in history: Bitcoin.

Bitcoin hardens under duress and challenge. Bitcoin's properties, qualities, and value have never waned one iota. Bitcoin proves itself to the market each time it climbs out of these bear markets to new highs.

Experiencing an average of 80% of your price valuation getting wiped out isn't fun. However, as history and cycles have proven, Bitcoin doesn't care. It's the exchanges, the FUD'sters, the media, and the scammers who care. They are the ones instigating so much havoc.

We will see this again and again. There will be brutal sell-offs, depression, and a loss of hope. But then there will be a re-education, re-focus, and renewed revelation of what Bitcoin offers.

It's all about Bitcoin, not crypto. It's all about self-custody, not exchange custody. Buy and hold Bitcoin. That's it. Bitcoin doesn't need you to do anything fancy with it. Bitcoin is already every investment product you have ever known or could want, wrapped into one with total security by and for you.

Unfortunately, paper gold never gets wiped out. This is part of the problem. It's like a slow, long scam that never flushes out the rehypothecation. It will always prevent gold from reaching a fair market value for something supposed to be a scarce asset.

Outside of the preppers or older generations, most want to avoid dealing with physical gold. So gold becomes an almost permanent, financialized paper product. It is why Bitcoin is better at being gold than gold.

If everyone who owns gold were to convert to Bitcoin, it would place Bitcoin's market price well over $500k per Bitcoin.

Real Estate has a worldwide market cap of over $350 trillion. Stocks are at $100 trillion. Bonds are over $400 trillion. Art and other collectibles are over $30 trillion. Add in gold's $12 trillion and there's roughly $900 trillion in global market value.

Most of that value is financialized, meaning those products are owned for their value appreciation, not their utility. Owners/investors would be happy to shift that value into something more liquid, less cumbersome, and more secure.

If (when) people allocate only 5% of their portfolio to Bitcoin, that will place Bitcoin's market price at over $2 million per coin. But again, if no one ever bought Bitcoin other than those who want a better version of gold, Bitcoin will reach above $500k.

Here's why this will eventually happen: Goldbugs and Bitcoiners think alike regarding sound money.

They agree money must be scarce. Gold is primarily scarce, but we don't know how much there really is. Bitcoin is programmatically scarce and viewable in real-time to the exact one-one hundred millionth of a Bitcoin.

They agree money must be durable. Gold will never expire. Bitcoin is code on a shared ledger that will live as long as the universe accepts math rules.

They agree money must be portable. People can only grab their gold bars and flee to another country with armored cars, security guards, or a magical way to cross borders in an airplane or ship without censorship and confiscation.

Bitcoin can travel without any friction. Whether .00000001 of a Bitcoin or 1 million Bitcoin, it can be moved anywhere on a phone, hidden in a microchip, or even in your memory with those magical seed words.

They agree money must be recognizable. Without an expert, most can't tell the difference between fake and real gold. Bitcoin is Bitcoin. There is no such thing as fake Bitcoin.

I take that back. There is fake Bitcoin. It's called crypto. And crypto is incompatible with Bitcoin's blockchain. Fortunately, crypto doesn't look or sound like Bitcoin. So again, you can recognize Bitcoin.

They agree money must be fungible. Gold requires an expert to tell you that ten 1 oz pieces are identical in value to one 10 oz piece. But anyone will gladly accept two transactions of 0.5 Bitcoin as happily as 1.

They agree money must have a high stock-to-flow. Gold's flow can change any time the price incentivizes more mining. Bitcoin has the most deterministic and exact schedule. And, of course, there is a finite ceiling to Bitcoin's stock. It ends at 21 million.

They agree money must represent sovereignty to the holder. Gold offers this to those who feel secure with a safe or hole in their backyard. Bitcoin takes liberty to an exponential level with math, code, and electricity to protect it from state or third-party interference.

They agree money must be decentralized. Money's purpose is so people can store and exchange energy with one another in the fairest method possible. If governments, states, or companies can bypass equality of money, then it is no longer money.

Most physical gold is stored in the same 10 banks worldwide that have always had it. Those banks are decentralized in theory but controlled by centralized institutions. So no. Bitcoin is the first fully decentralized money ever. The access is identical for a peasant in Vietnam as it is for the central bank of Italy.

They agree that, above all else, money must store value, for that is the actual definition of money. Money needs to be... money! Gold does a reasonably good job of value storage. Accessing that value when you need to is awkward. Bitcoin satisfies this hard money thesis without being physically hard. It carries your past energy forward in time without manipulation or debasement.

Both Bitcoin and gold compete for the same resource. They both absorb fiat as a way to store value with more integrity. If just one of these has a slight advantage, it will force the other to wither away.

Quite bluntly, gold is a relic. It belongs stuffed away in treasure chests on pirate ships guarded by cannons. To future generations, gold is a VCR. It is one for the history books or dusty pawn shops.

The best use-case for gold is to explain Bitcoin. But once you describe Bitcoin as digital gold, there's no need for gold.

No money system has ever been created since we've had the internet. That's hard to believe. We now finally have money on a distributed digital accounting system, much like the internet's users on a distributed network system.

The value proposition of the internet is that everyone has access. There is no walled garden for elites. Everyone can give or receive value. Everyone can participate all at once or not at all.

Money should be no different. Money should be accessible at all times, 24/7, for everyone, just like the internet.

Do you know a single person who doesn't use the internet? In time, you won't know anyone who doesn't use Bitcoin.

10

PROOF OF SATOSHI

"I must confess that my imagination refuses to see any sort of submarine doing anything but suffocating its crew and floundering at sea"

H.G. Wells, British Novelist, 1901

B itcoin's lack of any entity or person is what money has needed all these years. It was the missing piece that could finally make money fair. Because to have truly decentralized money requires that no one is in charge.

Whether government or not, any person or group can't have an ounce of power or influence over anyone else for pure and hard money - there can't be a singular voice, a hierarchy, or even a location. Any single point of contact for a protocol makes it centralized by definition.

It seems almost mystical, like a fairy-tale or sci-fi movie, that someone could remain anonymous for years; build a new monetary system that solved problems that mathematicians, scientists, and engineers said were unsolvable; and then make the final necessary sacrifice and vanish.

This person invented money and the piping for that money to flow to everyone in the world, taking no credit, compensation, adulation, or notoriety. And now the entire world knows about it.

"Satoshi Nakamoto" might represent one person, or it might be a group of people. In a move almost as brilliant as creating Bitcoin itself, Satoshi managed to keep his identity from the entire world, including the NSA and CIA, who have attempted to figure the mystery out (and offered rewards if anyone could).

Similar to other monumental inventions, Bitcoin didn't just pop up overnight.

Hundreds of cypherpunks, coders, engineers, and software developers have attempted to fix and improve electronic money for decades. In some ways, Bitcoin is simply an amalgamation of all the breakthroughs that came before it.

Once you dig into Bitcoin and how it works, you see why Satoshi's nonexistence was inevitable. It was always part of the plan. Although, as you'll see below, that plan may have been accelerated due to illness.

Marc Andreessen, owner of the largest VC firm, a16z, and famous for start-ups like Facebook, Twitter, Pinterest, and hundreds more, wanted to invent something like Bitcoin.

Instead Marc invented Netscape, which was the first internet browser to allow credit cards. We forget how it was once impossible to pay for things over the internet, or how you'd never punch in your credit card number on a website. Netscape changed that.

Marc is a serial entrepreneur who files patents, creates companies, and is a figurehead for everything he does. This would have never worked for Bitcoin - it required someone with no ego or showmanship.

Elon Musk and Peter Thiel also wanted to invent peer-to-peer digital money.

In a 1999 speech, Peter said, "When everybody has a phone connected to the internet, we could then use that phone to manage our own money and do payments back and forth with each other without the need for banks. And governments would not be able to stop it without taking down the entire internet."

But Elon and Peter couldn't figure out several issues: How do you secure the payment network and make it impenetrable to counterfeiters? How do you solve the slow settlement issues with banks?

Instead, they created PayPal and transferred the U.S. dollar back and forth on traditional bank rails. PayPal became a centralized, digital bank. Now, PayPal and its sister company, Venmo, offer Bitcoin. But they are no different than any commercial bank concerning limitations and custody.

Like Marc Andreesen, Elon Musk and Peter Thiel have prominent, public personas that sway markets. Money can't work with that level of influence.

Before Bitcoin, numerous protocols came close to solving digital money. Each one of them added unique code that helped Bitcoin evolve. None of them could reach full purity for all the properties money needs to have, especially decentralization, scarcity, and security from government or bad actors.

Over 100 years ago, Henry Ford wanted to create an "energy currency" separate from the state. He wanted something that the Fed couldn't print. He essentially wanted Bitcoin's "proof of work" before that was a concept.

Henry Ford said, "It is enough that people of the nation do not understand our banking and monetary system, for if they did, I believe there would be a revolution before tomorrow morning."

In the 1980s, computer scientist and cryptographer David Chaum proposed an electronic cash system. His project eventually became eCash. It's probably the first form of digital cash we've ever had. And for that, he is considered the godfather and creator of "cryptocurrency."

Dr. Adam Back developed Hashcash by inventing a "proof of work" system. He attempted to eliminate spam emails by making senders prove who they were via micropayments. He's mentioned in Satoshi's original white paper and was the second person to receive an email from Satoshi.

Later, Wei Dai's B-money and Nick Szabo's BitGold took these protocols a step further to combat inflation with digital scarcity and distribute across a global ledger.

Nick Szabo's BitGold brought us the closest to what Bitcoin is today. BitGold eliminated the middleman and made it decentralized.

PayPal couldn't figure out this aspect of how money could be in the hands of all the people rather than a "trusted" authority to manage the ledger. Decentralization was a critical step in having actual peer-to-peer money, not peer-to-company-to-government-to-company-to-peer money.

It is partially why names like Mark Zuckerberg or Elon Musk could never create Bitcoin. They want control. They make themselves the stars rather than the protocol. And their products and services are directly related to their personalities and decisions.

There's speculation that Nick Szabo is Satoshi (or one of a group making up "Satoshi"). Satoshi's message on the chat forums to other cryptographers was that he would use his initials for his first Bitcoin transaction. The first Bitcoin sent was signed with "NS," as in Nick Szabo.

But it should be noted that in Asian countries, initials are reversed, so "NS" could equally stand for Satoshi Nakamoto. On the other hand, there's no indication anywhere that Satoshi was Japanese based on his activity.

It's believed Satoshi was at times in Northern California and at times in Europe judging from time stamps and hours of the day on his email activity, Twitter posts, online chat forums, and cypherpunk groups.

It's also believed Satoshi worked partially as a postdoc or in some form of academia based on specific phrasing and formatting of his writings.

Satoshi released his white paper on October 31, 2008. He outlined the entire Bitcoin protocol with English phrasing, like, "bloody hard" and spelling the color gray the English way with G-R-E-Y.

Satoshi's first message on the Bitcoin blockchain referenced a story in The Times, an English newspaper. It read: "The Times 03/Jan/2009 Chancellor on brink of second bailout for banks." This was a reference to fiat's never-ending money printing and its devaluation of its citizens.

Bitcoin's origination was a peaceful protest against the banking bailouts from the Global Financial Crisis in America of 2008. It was in response to the bankruptcy of Lehman Brothers and the bailout of Merrill Lynch. But stamped in the blockchain is a reference to an English newspaper.

Nick Szabo is American. However, Dr. Adam Back is English. Could Satoshi have been a combination of the two? Both men adamantly deny that they are Satoshi, yet they are on many people's short-lists of top 5 contenders.

Then there's Hal Finney, another American computer scientist. Hal was a prominent cryptographer who was involved early on in the community. He received the very first email from Satoshi and helped test and troubleshoot what has now become Bitcoin.

A couple of months after Satoshi released the white paper, he sent the first 10 Bitcoin to Hal Finney. If I were testing out a new email program, I'd probably send myself an email from one address to another.

But analysts think it would be crazy and too time-consuming for Hal Finney to email himself for as long as Satoshi and Hal communicated online.

Then there's the oddity of Hal's neighbor, a Japanese man named Dorian Satoshi Nakamoto. Maybe Hal used his neighbor's name as his pseudonym. Or since Hal and the real Satoshi communicated so much, perhaps the real Satoshi learned of Hal's neighbor's name and adopted it.

The neighbor named Dorian Satoshi Nakamoto has denied he is Satoshi, and based on his background and work, no one questions that he is Bitcoin's Satoshi Nakamoto.

Unfortunately, Hal died in 2014 from complications of ALS. As tragic as that is, who better to keep a secret than someone dead?

Hal decided to cryo-preserve his body. And since Bitcoin is the first money of its kind ever to transcend time and space without energy loss, some think Hal could unfreeze (or have a head transplant) and punch in his memorized 24 words to access his Bitcoin one day.

If true, or even possible, Satoshi would never move his Bitcoin. He knows doing so would reveal who he is.

Finally, Len Sassaman is a well-respected cryptographer less known than everyone above. Len worked with and was instrumental in many cryptographic protocols like BitTorrent and key encryption (the basis of Bitcoin). And he also was on the internet task force for the internet's TCP/IP layer (another Bitcoin similarity).

Len lived in Northern California. But he also worked in academia in Belgium and researched under David Chaum, the godfather of cryptocurrency.

Here's why that's important:

Many of Len's posts and tweets show that he specifically used the phrase "bloody hard" when complaining about phone service. And he talked about his "grey beard" with the G-R-E-Y spelling.

Those occurrences explain why even though people think Satoshi is English, it could be Len who fits all of the other criteria.

The timestamps of Len's activity correlate directly with his time in San Francisco and later when he was in Belgium.

Satoshi's last message was posted in December 2010 and existed online until April 2011. He wrote, "there's more work to be done," but that Bitcoin is "in good hands."

Sadly, Len died at age 31 when he took his own life on July 3, 2011. Len had severe depression but also a life-long neurological disorder, just like Hal Finney. Hal died 3 years later.

Satoshi's final communication with other cryptographers was that he "moved on to other things," and that he "won't be around much longer."

It's possible (and my guess) that "Satoshi Nakamoto" is both Len and Hal. Both men worked together on Remailers, a private communication protocol that uses pseudonymous names. I could imagine both guys adopting Hal's neighbor's name and developing Bitcoin under it.

If my hunch is correct, aside from the sad loss of these two men, they have given the world one of the most important gifts ever - the separation of money and state. And with that as the goal, Satoshi's disappearance was built in. It was planned. Not that suicide was planned, but leaving Bitcoin so the world could accept it was imperative.

Satoshi is credited with inventing Bitcoin. But really, he was the first person to implement and synthesize all of these prior protocols and inventions from other cryptographers together in a way that made Bitcoin work.

Henry Ford didn't invent tires. He didn't invent the transmission or the internal combustion engine. But Ford knew by combining these breakthroughs, he could create the automobile, for which he is credited as the inventor.

Satoshi knew how important it is to keep money perfect and uncontaminated. He didn't want anyone, including himself, to have an unfair advantage over the most perfect money ever created. And for that reason, I suspect he threw away the keys to his Bitcoin stash of 1 million Bitcoin.

If Satoshi were to have access to his Bitcoin, he would be ridiculously rich. At one point, he was the 12th richest person in the world per the price of Bitcoin. And in the future, he'll be the world's richest person.

Either way, whether dead or alive, it makes no difference since Satoshi can no longer affect Bitcoin more than anyone else. The protocol was released and is now owned by the people, not him, just as he wanted it.

Satoshi made Bitcoin simple, lean, and slow enough to accommodate any financial activity built on top of it. He designed it to be the only protocol sufficient to secure the world's wealth. This way, no new decisions need to be made.

Bitcoin doesn't need any upgrades, improvements, seed rounds of funding, buy-outs, mergers, or any mechanics we are accustomed to from companies run by boardrooms and investors.

There are volunteer engineers and coders, some of whom worked with Satoshi, who continue to stress-test Bitcoin and work on technical aspects to improve parts of Bitcoin. But all of these suggestions must be approved by everyone (nodes), including you and me.

Even the multi-billion dollar mega-corporation with political influence has no more powerful vote than yours. This is what proof of work gives us over proof of stake.

This process was highlighted during a period between 2015 to 2017 when well-funded Bitcoin companies (like Coinbase) wanted to increase the block size of transactions to speed it up. Bitcoin users knew this would make it more difficult for the average person to monitor Bitcoin on their home laptops.

Even though Coinbase and other companies spent hundreds of millions to campaign to change Bitcoin, the users rejected it. The people, not the mega-corporation, won.

This is why there are "forks" like Bitcoin Cash (BCH) and Bitcoin Satoshi Vision (BSV). Anyone can copy Bitcoin. Since it's open-source, the code is free to use and share. Doge and Litecoin are two examples. Both copied the code and rebranded it.

But forks and copies don't mean users will follow, regardless of how influential or well-funded those users are.

Satoshi built Bitcoin to purposefully be able to withstand attacks and pressure from outside forces. It's not meant to do much of anything outside of being a solid, dependable accounting ledger.

But even a simple ledger in cyberspace is a challenge when anything can be copied, including your money.

Traditional finance companies have to monitor and manually change their ledgers to ensure that if someone sends $10 to someone, their account is debited and the other person's account is credited. Otherwise, that person can spend the $10 again - a double-spend.

This simple process requires a lot of trust, energy, and expenditure among finance companies. It's why they need a central authority. There is no other way around this.

It was impossible to solve this double-spend issue and coincide with decentralization cryptographically. Before Bitcoin, people said it could not be done if the ledger were equally distributed where anyone else could change it.

Central banks and counterfeiters both double-spend. A central bank adds numbers to a computer screen. A counterfeiter physically duplicates paper money.

In both cases, the newly created currency absorbs and sucks out value from the old dollars users earn. Those who work for money are debased due to the double-spend of money printing or forgery.

The digital verse accelerates the ease with which this double-spend can scale. Imagine a Microsoft Word document you spent hours working on, writing, editing, and polishing for its intended purpose. You now email it to its destination. You just double-spent.

The minute you sent your document, you and the recipient had the exact same file. It's on your computer. It's on their computer. There is no difference. That recipient, in turn, can forward your document to other parties. And so on. An unlimited number of people can have an exact copy. Yet, you were the only one who did the work.

The original document is your proof of work. But because it could be double-spent, it took that proof away. Once it is copied, there is no discernment between your proof-of-work and a copy's double-spending of your work. The effect is no different than a central bank or counterfeiter.

Thus, for money, rather than a word document or JPEG, Satoshi Nakamoto needed to create an airtight system where a double-spend was impossible at any level for any reason. And he had to do this in a fully decentralized system. Otherwise, Bitcoin would need to have a leader.

Satoshi had to figure this out before he could exit.

11

PROOF OF KEYS

"Rock n' Roll will be gone by June."

Variety Magazine, 1955

To explain how Satoshi solved the double-spend, let's have some "friends" join us.

A group of friends hangs out at a local coffee shop in New York City to discuss money and finance. Due to various reasons, the group decides to exit the traditional banking system and set up a shared spreadsheet hosted in the cloud.

Monica sends $50 to Ross.

Next row, Rachel sends $75 to Chandler.

Next row, Chandler sends $30 to Joey. And so on.

At the end of the week, the group tallies everything up and settles their balances with each other. Some have to kick money into the pot, and others get money out of it.

But everyone begins questioning how safe or private this is with their money on a cloud-based system. Can't they log onto the Google spreadsheet and change the balances?

Monica has the solution to their concerns based on something she found online from a mysterious stranger's post. Following the stranger's instructions, she asks everyone to create their own digital wallet.

Each Bitcoin wallet is secured (backed up) by a *seed phrase*. These are those 12 to 24 words mentioned throughout the book. You can think of these words as "seeds" in that they grow the cryptographic wallet when planted together in the correct sequence. Or, in the case of loss, regrow it.

Each of the friends begins assembling their seed words to create their wallets. They can use random generators, dice, or choose their own words if they come from a specific list of 2,048 available choices.

If you search "Bip39 word list" online, you'll find all 2,048 available words. An example of 12 words from that list might look like this:

Idea Hammer Nature Yellow Valley Tiger Roast Panda Avocado Island Sentence Unveil.

At first, it might seem limiting that the 24 words which comprise a wallet come from only 2,048 words. Couldn't someone guess your seed words with enough guesses? Chandler and Joey think they know Monica well enough to figure out words someone like her would pick.

On the one hand, this is why it's best to use a random generator to pick them for you. There's less chance for human bias and preference. On the other hand, here's what it would take for Chandler and Joey to guess Monica's seed words:

The guys would arrive at a warehouse, Warehouse #1, that Monica built. Inside there are 2,048 doors. The guys have to choose the one and only door that advances them to the next warehouse, Warehouse #2. There's a 99.95% chance they'll choose the wrong door. That's 2,047 ways to lose - only 1 way to win.

But let's say they get lucky in Warehouse #1, open the door, and enter Warehouse #2. Now, Chandler and Joey are faced with another set of 2,048 doors. And once again, they have a 99.95% chance of picking the wrong one.

Between the 2 warehouses, there is only a 0.0023% chance they'll get both correct doors. Remember, the sequence is critical. The guys couldn't have chosen Warehouse #2's door first and then Warehouse #1's door second.

This process goes on for 24 warehouses deep! Each contains 2,048 doors, and Monica's wallet lives in the last one in Warehouse #24.

This produces a probability astronomically inconceivable to the human brain because it is 40 digits long: 5,444,517,870,735,015,415,413,993,71 8,908,291,383,296.00.

The chances of the guys guessing Monica's seed phrase to her wallet is 1 in 5 duodecillion 444 undecillion 517 decillion 870 nonillion 735 octillion 15 septillion 415 sextillion 413 quintillion 993 quadrillion 718 trillion 908 billion 291 million 383 thousand 296.

Even if Monica tells her 24 words to Chandler and Joey, but not the correct order of the words, the guys would never figure it out. It would still take them 620 sextillion guesses to find the proper sequence of Monica's seed words.

In addition, there are optional *passphrases* on top of these 24 words that one can engage if one desires. This passphrase becomes a "25th word," but that isn't from any specific list and doesn't even have to be a word.

The 25th word can be a sentence, paragraph, or anything incomprehensible, like an extremely long string of numbers and letters. The user can make this phrase anything they want. And exact spacing, punctuation, and capitalization are critical.

The odds are incalculable because of how indefinite this last word can be.

With that explanation, the group feels comfortable that their money is safe. They each create their 24 seed words and hide them from prying eyes.

Next, from their seed words, they each generate a *secret key* and a *public key*. These are the two keys generated by each set of seed words. It is essentially their wallet. The wallet holds these two keys.

The public key allows anyone to produce a *public address*, like an apartment address, where others on the ledger can send money. Money can only travel to a public address, not from it. This is why it's public.

The secret key allows anyone to send money out of that wallet. It is the key that a user will never show to anyone under any circumstance whatsoever. Anyone with this secret key can send all the money out of a wallet to whomever they want.

With each of their two keys - the public and secret keys - the group of friends can send and receive whenever they want on this shared online ledger.

Since Ross owes Rachel $200, he asks her to text him her public address so he can send the funds. This part is similar to transacting on PayPal or Venmo. But there's one unique difference.

Whereas with Venmo or PayPal, there is just one public address for each user, like @Rachel, essentially unlimited Bitcoin public addresses can be generated from one public key (actually 4,294,967,296 public addresses for any one Bitcoin public key).

Rachel uses her public key to generate one of these many public addresses. It doesn't matter which one she gives Ross, as they all lead back to that one public key.

Like Rachel's 10 different purses, the contents of her public addresses all funnel back to her ownership. She can swap money from purse to purse or address to address, but she is still the "key" to all those containers. They are just surrogates of her.

By generating a new public address each time Rachel wants to receive money, she hides her transaction history and balance from the sender. Just as if Ross were to open one of Rachel's purses, he'd only see what was in that specific purse - cash and receipts - not the collective of all 10 purses.

With Rachel's public address, Ross knows where to send the $200 he owes her. But what if right after Ross sends it, Rachel claims she has yet to receive it or received $200 from her mom, not Ross? It's her word against his since there's no bank to mediate.

Digital Signatures solve this. They are composed of three ingredients.

1. The transaction message.

2. The secret key

3. A random number.

Those three inputs equate to Ross' digital signature. It announces to everyone that it is indeed Ross who is sending this money to Rachel.

Joey can't recreate Ross' signature. Chandler can't say he's Ross. And Rachel can't say that her mom sent her the money when Ross' unique digital signature is present.

Let's review these 3 ingredients as Ross makes his transaction with Rachel.

Assume the first ingredient, the *transaction message*, is "Ross sends $200 to Rachel," which we'll shorten to R200R for the sake of illustration.

The second ingredient is Ross' secret key. That key is *****.

Since only Ross knows his secret key, that's all we can see. In reality, it's a string of 256 ones and zeros, but he isn't sharing it with anyone. He uses it as one of the 3 ingredients to create his digital signature.

Finally, Ross adds the third ingredient, a random number, 11111. This, too, can be anything.

The math for Ross' digital signature now looks something like this:

R200R (transaction message) +

* * * * * (Ross' secret key) +

11111 (a random number) +

= ROSS9

Ross now has his one-time digital signature, ROSS9, for this specific transaction to Rachel. It's a one-time use because it is tied to the particular transaction message and the random number.

As basic as this computation is with only three inputs, You can't reverse engineer it. It prevents a hacker from ever trying to figure out Ross' secret key or tamper with it.

It's as if Ross is making a protein shake with these 3 ingredients. You can't undo Ross' shake back into the banana, peanut butter, and milk he blended. Once blended, there's no way Ross can get the banana out of the shake and back into its original form in the banana peel.

If any of these ingredients are changed just one iota, like making his random number 11112 instead of 11111, the final output will be completely different and random.

On the Bitcoin network, these elements form a cryptographic number so unfathomably large (2^{256}) that it would be easier for someone to find a specific hidden grain of sand somewhere in the entire universe (including every ocean floor on every planet) than figure out Ross' digital signature.

The probability of finding this grain of sand produces a number with 77 zeros behind it. The human brain can't comprehend this large of a number. It prevents anyone from duplicating or forging another's digital signature.

The friends now know this is Ross because of his digital signature. But how do they verify that he has $200 to send to Rachel in the first place? Since we are in the digital verse, it is easy to duplicate or copy numbers. There's that *double-spend problem*.

As clunky and time-consuming as it sounds, the friends must scan through and see all of Ross' past transactions. Everything Ross has already sent or received, from the beginning until now, will total up to his proper balance. It's a reconciliation to confirm how much he has at this exact moment in time before the transaction is allowed.

The friends go through the ledger and see that Ross started this wallet with a $1,000 deposit and then sent four payments of $100 each to Monica, Rachel, Chandler, and Joey. So there is currently $600 remaining, which is enough for Ross to send $200 to Rachel.

This transaction history of a user's Bitcoin is literally what Bitcoin is. Bitcoin is the list of the past transitions that the actual Bitcoin incurred to arrive where it is at any moment in time.

Let me further explain.

Bitcoin obviously isn't really a "coin." It's an accounting statement. But rather than represent a specific amount, like 1 Bitcoin, the value you send on the Bitcoin network is a complete list of sent and received transactions that equate to that specific Bitcoin.

A more accurate name for Bitcoin would be something like Digital Accounting History. That's a terrible name, obviously, but more descriptive of what Bitcoin is.

Look at these 4 lines below:

Mined 3 Bitcoin.

Sent 2 Bitcoin to Dad.

Received 4 Bitcoin from Sister.

Sent 4 Bitcoin to Mom.

Those 4 lines could be the 1 Bitcoin someone sends to another person. The total of those transactions equals 1 Bitcoin.

All Bitcoin, every Bitcoin, every fraction of a Bitcoin down to a single Satoshi contains the entire history of that Bitcoin from when it was first generated (mined) to where it is today, sitting in a wallet.

It would be like pulling a dollar out of your pocket and seeing where it's been before you had it. What transactions did it go through since it came off the printing press until it arrived in your pocket?

This history of every Bitcoin transaction is how Satoshi solved the double-spend problem. No trust is required to accept a balance on a statement. All that is necessary is lickety-split math.

Everyone on the Bitcoin network conducts an audit at the speed of light. The result is "True" or "False." Funds are available, or they are not.

It's impossible that all of the hundreds of thousands of users on the Bitcoin network around the world would simultaneously miscalculate a person's transactions to allow someone to double-spend.

If someone doesn't have the funds, a user on the network will raise their hand and say, "False." No referee is needed because everyone is a referee.

Traditional banks don't come close to this level of scrutiny and verification, let alone the need for trust. Mistakes are made, and we are forced to reconcile statements at the end of every month.

Retail banks base their accounting on credits and debits - promises. Not the transfer of actual money (final settlement). Accounts get overdrawn, transactions are sometimes double-spent, and minimum balances and fees are incurred to compensate for these issues.

Back to our friends - the group has confirmed Ross has the available funds. He can't double-spend. And they confirmed that it is actually Ross from his digital signature.

There is a final step of verification that proves both Ross' public and secret keys come from his wallet. It happens automatically since his secret and public key share the same DNA. They are both created from his 24 words.

Again, he doesn't show his secret key. But by showing his public key, he can prove it is his secret key that he is using.

It's like confirming with blood and DNA tests that one set of identical twins (Ross' public key) is from a set of parents (Ross' wallet). Once established, one can safely deduce that the other twin (Ross' secret key) is also from the same parents.

Now the group knows Ross' two keys were generated from his wallet (from his seed words). The transaction is officially verified. Off it goes!

The friends, however, overlook one big problem. They may have removed the bank and solved the double-spend problem but still rely on a centrally controlled, online spreadsheet.

The group has to trust the spreadsheet doesn't get hacked, deleted, banned, locked out, etc. It's on a centralized server, so it is prone to centralized activity. This is why the 6th friend, Phoebe, has not joined this experiment. She thinks the friends are crazy for trusting their money to an open system.

12

PROOF OF DECENTRALIZATION

"A rocket will never be able to leave the Earth's atmosphere."

New York Times, 1936

The *Byzantine Generals Problem* is a popular game theory exercise. It stems from a story where numerous generals of different allied armies prepare to attack the ancient Greek city of Byzantium.

But so many separate sets of armies and soldiers need to coordinate. How can they trust that there isn't a spy or bad actor in their ranks giving inaccurate or deceitful information?

These cooperating armies know they can conquer Byzantium, but only if they attack simultaneously. A united bombardment, all at once, is necessary to overcome Byzantium's strong defense.

If just one of the united armies attacks 10 minutes too early (or 10 minutes too late), it will alert Byzantium with a warning to overcome the other invading armies.

The armies need a *consensus* on when to attack. But how do they achieve unity in a trustless way? Just one spy posing as a messenger from one general to another can give false info on the time to attack.

The remedy to this problem has always been a central authority. But with that also comes censorship, permission, and the need to trust. It is still the solution today for every financial product or system, including altcoins.

Satoshi finally solved these problems to make money perfect, fairly distributed, decentralized, and immune to bad actors.

His solution to the Byzantine Generals Problem was implementing a proof of work protocol into Bitcoin's code. This protocol achieves consensus amongst strangers, no matter who they are, good or bad.

A proof of work system motivates all participants toward the same outcome. All one can do in a proof of work system is the work itself. There's nothing else available to do. One chooses to work or not. And by working, it leads to truth.

To illustrate this proof of work system, let's return to our friends in New York.

Monica instructs everyone to download a copy of the group's shared online spreadsheet and save it to their personal computers. She then deletes the master Google account, so nothing is online with a third party.

Hearing this, Phoebe finally joins the other 5 friends since she no longer has to worry about a centralized point of failure or privacy. She, too, downloads a copy to have the whole ledger on her computer.

But now all 6 friends must keep 6 separate sets of accurate records on their personal computers. Without a cloud-based system, it's burdensome to ensure each person has identical versions every time there's a new transaction.

Since the guys don't want the hassle of updating their own ledgers, the girls take on the responsibility. Monica, Rachel, and Phoebe all verify transactions to confirm they are legit. They do this by following the steps outlined in the previous chapter - checking digital signatures and public keys.

But now Ross, Chandler and Joey each have mismatched and outdated ledgers. Only the girls' versions of the ledger hold the truth.

This problem compounds when dozens of more New Yorkers join this system. Those who start with copies of one of the guys' spreadsheets don't match that of the girls' spreadsheets'.

This overwhelms Monica, Rachel, and Phoebe. It's a full-time job to verify transactions and then text everyone else to update their personal spreadsheets with the latest transactions. And there's no way of confirming the accuracy of others.

With delays, errors, and missed messages, it's a complete mess. So the original group of 6 friends takes their argument to the coffee shop downstairs to figure out a better system.

A computer programmer named Satoshi overhears their squabble. He leans in and asserts that he has the solution to their problems.

Satoshi whispers, "Let's play a game."

He explains to the group that whoever wins this new game is rewarded with a large amount of internet money magically deposited into the winner's account. It won't take away from anyone else's fiat money because it is an entirely separate and alternate money system that he calls "Bitcoin."

Anyone can be a contestant. But everyone doesn't need to be one. The game will take place as long as there is just one contestant.

As soon as a contestant wins the game, and thus Bitcoin, they can sell it for U.S. dollars or hold onto it - their choice.

The goal of the contest is simple.

Each contestant takes the most recent *pending transactions* that the girls have just verified and assembles them into a group called a *block*. Technically, each Bitcoin block can hold up to 2,000 transactions but only needs to contain 1 if activity is slow.

Currently, the girls have 15 transactions ready to go. They verified them by analyzing the users' digital signatures and public keys.

At this point, Satoshi wants the girls to send those 15 transactions to all potential contestants rather than to all users. In other words, rather than send these off to every single person in this new money system, send the new transactions to only those who want to be contestants.

Part of the reason there are inaccurate and inconsistent versions of the ledger floating around is that it's a nuisance to update it after every transaction. Even though the girls feel that their versions of the ledger are perfect, it doesn't mean others are motivated to keep those same records for themselves.

Satoshi's contest fixes this problem.

A new contest begins every 10 minutes, so there are endless chances to win. Therefore, there are 6 contests per hour, every hour, 24/7. There can only be one winner for each contest, but there is no limit to how many contests one can enter. There is no second place. And there is no advantage to who you are or where you are.

To demonstrate, Satoshi runs the first contest for the group as the sole contestant. But he agrees not to cash out the Bitcoin reward since no one is competing with him. That wouldn't be fair. He doesn't want this new system to be tainted by the same manipulation and privilege of centralized banking.

One by one, Satoshi goes through the 15 transactions that the girls have already verified on behalf of all the users. He compiles pending deposits, pending withdrawals, and pending transfers into a block. Check, check, and check.

As a contestant, Satoshi is assembling "sentences" that the girls have sent him so that he can make a "paragraph." In this example, there are 15 sentences.

Once Satoshi completes his block, he adds his own unique sentence (transaction) at the end that proves he, Satoshi, assembled the block. This last transaction is called the *proof of work number.*

Here's the catch, the conundrum, and the contest, all in one:

Satoshi has no idea what the proof of work number is. There are no hints, hacks, or any way to game what that number might be. The only way to arrive at this number is to guess.

This process of figuring out the target proof of work number is the contest itself. Assembling the block is relatively easy for a contestant. But figuring out a number from an extensive set of possibilities is a complete lottery.

Pretend I said, "Pick a number between 1 and 10,000, and I will give you 6.25 Bitcoin once you land on the number I've chosen. You can guess as many times as you want. Go."

Your only option is to start shouting out as many numbers as possible and as fast as possible. Once you hit it, I know you did the work. I know you must have yelled out a bunch of numbers and exerted energy because how else could you have landed on my number without making a lot of guesses?

Can you guess the number on the first guess? Sure. But you could also spend all day making guesses depending on the range's size. What if I said the number I was thinking of was between 1 and 900 million?

Thus Satoshi guesses repeatedly until he finds the proof of work number. Bam. He completes the block.

With the winning proof of work number at the end of the block, Satoshi is on his way to earning a nice Bitcoin reward. But there are still a few more steps that must happen to ensure no mistakes.

Satoshi sends his completed block back over to the girls to validate. Whereas Monica, Rachel, and Phoebe initially *verified* the 15 pending transactions, now they can *validate* them and check his last winning proof of work number. They want to make sure he didn't try to alter or double-spend any of the 15 transactions.

Once validated, the girls send the block out to all the other network users. By now, at least 500 New Yorkers are using this new money system. So the girls broadcast to everyone that this new version is the official version since it has the latest block that won the contest.

Once a majority of other users confirm this new block, a consensus is reached. Then (and only then) Satoshi is issued his Bitcoin reward. It automatically deposits right into his public address. Cha-ching! The contest is officially over for block #1.

The only way Bitcoin can enter the supply is through these contests. Contestants win the Bitcoin reward and spend it in the economy where others acquire it. It's similar to how gold enters the supply via miners.

Gold must also be verified, validated, and put into a block (a brick of gold). Miners then sell their gold into the economy to make money for their proof of work.

As a reminder, it is known with unmitigated mathematical certainty that only 6.25 Bitcoin are brought into the total supply every 1 block (or 10 minutes) if it's before 2024's Halving event. This 6.25 Bitcoin is the contest reward. The contestant who wins the 6.25 Bitcoin will sell it into the economy to make a profit.

After 2024's halving event, 3.125 Bitcoin is the reward for each contest. After 2028's halving event, 1.5625 is the reward. And so on, until all 21 million Bitcoin are in circulation by 2140.

Each Halving event occurs every 210,000 blocks. Since each block takes 10 minutes on average, that becomes 1,458 days or every 4 years. This creates the 4-year cycles of Bitcoin's bull and bear markets.

Compare Bitcoin's issuance schedule to fiat's, which inflates at whim, without notice, and unfairly distributes. Each time more money enters the supply, it increases, and we have yet to learn by how much until after the fact.

Bitcoin's proof of work is crucial and significant to its value proposition. Without proof of work, Bitcoin would be just another crypto project. It would be fiat all over again.

Proof of work makes Bitcoin valuable against human manipulation in a decentralized system. The most moral and ethical things in life are decentralized. It's centralization that taints the clear signal of decentralization.

Religion is decentralized, denominational churches are not. Health is decentralized, the medical and insurance industry is not. Education is decentralized, school systems are not. Bitcoin is decentralized, central banks and fiat currencies are not.

The wheel, fire, and the number zero are all decentralized. They all only do one thing, which is why they do so much. And they do it without the trust of a third party. The singularity of these systems gives them unlimited applications across every industry. Bitcoin is no different.

The Bitcoin network does one thing: It sends value from address A to address B. But it will do that with immutability and security, ensuring it is final and done. This is literally all Bitcoin does, which is why it does so much. But this can only work when decentralized.

Now that Satoshi has demonstrated the first block's contest, he makes it easier for everyone else going forward. He releases software called Bitcoin Core, that is available at Bitcoin.org.

Bitcoin's software is open-source. It's available to scrutinize, tear apart, copy, or do whatever anyone wants. There is nothing secretive about it. It's quite simple to view and understand.

The Bitcoin Core software will automate everything the girls have been doing by hand. It will check for digital signatures and transaction messages and confirm public keys to prevent double-spending. And it will do it within fractions of a second.

Monica, Rachel, and Phoebe all download the Bitcoin Core software. They can work smarter and have their lives back. Satoshi smiles and says, "Congrats. You are now officially *nodes.*"

Anyone who verifies transactions and validates blocks on the Bitcoin network is a node. They don't personally have to do anything other than run the software on their computer. Turn it on, go about their day.

The incentive for nodes on the Bitcoin network is several-fold:

1. Nodes help keep the network secure. They confirm that transactions are accurate and that anyone attempting to double-spend is kicked off. Although there's no direct monetary gain, the incentive is that you personally know whether everything is accurate and true. Nodes like to say, "Trust, but verify."

2. Privacy. You're completely outside of the banking or any centralized system when you're a node. You can send, receive, and verify your own Bitcoin transactions. You are literally your own bank

without any custody or third-party services.

3. Nodes contribute to the overall value of the network via decentralization. They contribute to fairness and equality. Each new node that joins adds yet another copy of the same ledger and distributes the network's reach.

4. Nodes help increase Bitcoin's value through all of the above. So from this perspective, the monetary gain is in a node's contribution to increasing its price.

Now it's time for the next contest - block #2.

Satoshi explains that anyone who wants to be a contestant must update their personal ledger to an exact copy of the previous block's winner. In this case, the ledger of a potential contestant would need to match Satoshi's since he won the last block, block #1.

The Bitcoin Core software achieves this by downloading the latest confirmed block. And since each block is linked to all prior blocks, having the most recent one gives you the entire blockchain or the entire ledger (same thing).

This ingenious yet straightforward process solves the decentralization problem of non-matching ledgers among nodes. It keeps the one valid version of the ledger moving forward in time block after block, with all other versions discarded.

Suddenly, Ross, Chandler, and Joey find the motivation to update their ledgers, just as Satoshi imagined. They have no other choice if they want to attempt to win Bitcoin.

With Bitcoin's easy-to-run software, the girls are no longer the only nodes on the network. Now there are hundreds of nodes, all verifying transactions and validating blocks - essentially hundreds of accountants and auditors protecting the truth of the ledger.

For this next contest, block #2, the nodes have supplied 250 transactions. The guys each compete against each other to assemble these transactions into blocks. They then make as many guesses as quickly as possible to find the proof of work number.

Remember, finding this proof of work number is the contest. Anyone can assemble these blocks since the nodes have already verified them. But finding the proof of work number takes energy to guess and guess again until you get it right. It takes work.

At this point, Satoshi reveals to the guys that instead of calling them "contestants," he will call them *miners*. Although they indeed compete to win a reward, they are essentially mining for Bitcoin.

The guys input potential proof of work numbers over and over until someone wins. With the help of his pet monkey's fast finger, Ross arrives at a proof of work number that completes the block.

Ross follows the same procedure as Satoshi to claim his Bitcoin reward with the previous block. He sends block #2 back to all the nodes to validate his work. The nodes see his proof of work number and confirm the block. Once enough *confirmations* come back to reach a consensus, Ross receives his bitcoin reward.

The contest for block #3 begins. Rinse and repeat. 10 minutes at a time. Tick tock. Next block.

This proof of work system is part of Satoshi's solution to the Byzantine Generals Problem. By forcing all soldiers from the allied armies to prove their work, bad actors become obsolete. Bad actors are more incentivized to join, do the work, and receive the reward than attempt to derail it. Thus bad actors become good.

Bitcoin's proof of work is an impenetrable mechanism that doesn't have to trust good or evil. It makes no difference. It simply requires proof that someone is securing this accounting ledger to record only legit transactions. Everything else is denied so it never makes it into the blockchain.

The allied soldiers were asking what time they should strike the city. But what they needed to ask was at what point they should strike. The answer to that question is when the proof of work is evident.

13

PROOF OF DIFFICULTY

"Children just aren't interested in Witches and Wizards."

from a publishing executive to J.K. Rowling, 1996

After Ross won the mining reward for block #2, tens of thousands of new users joined this decentralized monetary system. Some want to participate in these mining contests and attempt to earn Bitcoin. But most want to save in a system without permission, surveillance, intermediaries, and especially inflation.

Mining doesn't always pencil out. Yet it will always incentivize its process. The reward is attractive, but there's no guarantee you'll win. And there are computer set-up and electricity costs.

This is one reason Monica, Rachel, and Phoebe decide to remain nodes and not bother mining. They want to increase the integrity of their money and secure the network. But they know mining is a lottery.

Chandler and Joey, however, want to team up and game the system as miners. They realize if they can increase the number of guesses they can make during a contest, they have a better chance of winning. They didn't stand a chance against Ross' fast pet monkey. So Chandler and Joey take out a loan and buy a dozen ASIC computers.

An Application Specific Integrated Circuit (ASIC) is the small computer miners use to search for the proof of work number that will win the contest. An ASIC does absolutely nothing but comes up with guesses faster than a standard computer.

The world's fastest quantum supercomputers ever built are slower than an ASIC computer when rotating through numbers. Whereas supercomputers solve complicated math problems, ASIC computers only flip through numbers at lightning speed until they find one that wins. It's essentially a shoe-box sized number generator.

An ASIC can compute up to 400 quintillion hashes (guesses) in a second. Ross' pet monkey doesn't stand a chance against Chandler and Joey with an ASIC, let alone 12 of them. At the same time, Ross still has a chance.

Chance is an essential aspect of Bitcoin's technology. It prevents a takeover of any well-funded corporation or entity. Since every miner has an equal opportunity of winning, regardless of how fast their computer is, it prevents outside influence.

Satoshi didn't want any nation-state, billionaire, or conglomerate to have any benefit over one person. He didn't want mathematicians or engineers to have an advantage with algorithms or formulas. He didn't want states or governments to have preference due to technology. Thus he implemented this agnostic trial and error system to get the mining reward.

Every block's contest is a lottery. When Joey and Chandler turn on their ASICs to out-compete Ross, they effectively buy more lottery tickets. Having more tickets costs them more but gives them better odds. Even so, anyone with a single lottery ticket can still win.

If you look at actual winners of state lotteries, you'll note that rarely is it some pool or corporation. As popular as office lottery pools are, the winner is typically some random person who bought a single ticket on a whim.

For the mining lottery, imagine a huge 500-sided dice. It can roll a 1 or a 500, or any number in between. Assume Ross has 1 dice, equivalent to the speed of his pet monkey. With their superfast ASIC computers, Chandler and Joey have the equivalent of 12 dice.

Now, assume the proof of work number for block #3's contest must be less than 5. Any miner can win this contest by rolling a 1, 2, 3, or 4 with a 500-sided dice.

This is closer to how the proof of work number technically works. It's more of a range of numbers that can win than any specific number. It could almost be called the "proof of work range" rather than "number."

In this scenario, Ross (or his pet monkey) would keep rolling his large 500-sided dice, hoping to turn up anything below 5. It could take a while with so many options. Mathematically, any dice has a 0.8% chance of finding 1, 2, 3, or 4 out of 500 possible choices.

Meanwhile, Chandler and Joey must work with the identical 500-sided dice as everyone else. But because of their *hash power* (12 dice instead of 1), they can make 12 guesses in the same time span that Ross and his monkey are making 1 guess. Still, every dice has an equal probability of winning.

After every guess (roll of the dice), a miner is no closer to winning than after 31 trillion guesses. This isn't an exaggeration. A miner could have made 30.9 trillion guesses, and the final guess is no closer than the person who flips on their computer and makes a single guess and wins.

The contest for block #3 begins. And once again, nodes quickly verify transactions and feed them to the miners. All competing miners assemble them into blocks and start hashing out their proof of work number. They all hope to roll anything below a 5. The first one to do so wins the Bitcoin block reward.

Within 1 minute, Chandler and Joey find the proof of work number before anyone else. Their block #3 is sent back to the nodes. The nodes quickly validate the block for accuracy and then confirm that the proof of work number is correct. It fits within the acceptable range.

The Bitcoin reward for block #3 automatically deposits into Chandler and Joey's account, and the next contest for block #4 begins.

Because these blocks all stack on top of each other, each new one further cements the prior one, making the older blocks even more secure from hacks or tampering. Blocks become completely impenetrable and uneditable under the "weight" of newer blocks.

If you think of a stack of dining plates, as the pile grows, plates closest to the bottom become more challenging to access and eventually impossible. Now pretend a small piece of each lower plate glues to a small part of the upper plate. They become fused rather than just sitting on top of each other.

Bitcoin blocks form a *blockchain* when the footer of one block becomes the header of the next one, and so on. You can only begin to assemble a block for a new blockchain by including the footer from the prior one.

If a criminal wanted to respend 10 Bitcoin that he had already spent, he would have to go back in time to that specific block where he spent the 10 Bitcoin and undo his one transaction. Then, he'd have to reassemble that past block, re-win the contest with an accurate proof of work number, and quickly win every block after that until he catches up to the present.

Since all these blocks link in the blockchain, criminals can't jump to and adjust the one block they want to falsify. They must travel through every single "plate" up to the top of the stack, re-winning every single contest.

This almost impossible task prevents bad actors from counterfeiting or double-spending, which is why it has never happened (and never will), as much as people try every single day.

Here's what it would take to attempt this deception:

A bad actor would have to invest a minimum of several billions of dollars in computing power (think thousands upon thousands of ASICs) for the chance to win a series of contests in a row as far back as the single transaction that he wants to undo or cheat. Against all odds of all other miners all over the world rolling those identical "dice," he'd have to be sure he won every single block, or his plan would be foiled.

As of publishing, it would take over $20 billion in computing power to control 51% of the mining network. On top of that, it would require an additional $15 billion just in electricity. So for $35 billion, a bad actor can have the chance to double-spend their Bitcoin before the other nodes kick him off.

If the targeted block a criminal wanted to manipulate occurred just 24 hours ago, that bad actor would have to win 144 contests in a row - every single 10-minute block. But the computing power of all other miners prevents this from happening. And millions of ASICs are running from every corner of the world.

Miners make it difficult due to speed and power. But it's the nodes who secure the network by authorization. Even in the ridiculously infinitesimal scenario a bad actor goes back in time and re-wins hundreds of blocks, the nodes won't accept it. Remember, the nodes must confirm the blocks and reach a consensus to accept them.

A bad actor would have to convince the majority of the nodes on the network to validate his new blockchain as the true one and reject the current one they've all been working on. It means more than 51% of other nodes (a consensus) would have to agree that they have all made a terrible mistake and that this newly presented blockchain, undoing an expenditure of 10 Bitcoin in the past, is the one they should accept.

See why Bitcoin is impenetrable? See why it will never be hacked?

Critics surmise that some evil nation, like North Korea, could amass computing power and hack the network (believe me, they are trying). But those critics fail to understand that the nodes, not the miners, secure the network. It is understandable when some of the biggest companies and banks in the world have all been hacked.

Over 140 million U.S. citizens, almost half the population, had their social security numbers exposed when the credit agency Equifax was hacked. The Pentagon has been hacked. And even products like pacemakers, baby monitors, and Jeeps have all been hacked and taken over.

Satoshi wisely distributed the authorization and security to the nodes, not the miners. He removed the possibility that any one bad actor or group of bad actors could outvote the good actors. The incentive is to be good.

It is we the people (the nodes) who decide. We are the ultimate security of the network, not the miners. Our consensus becomes the rule over any rulers.

If someone sends you Bitcoin, you have Bitcoin. No one can return in time and erase that due to its proof of work system. It is the most secure method of storing money that has ever existed. Thus mining energy isn't wasted but rather put to good use, protecting the integrity of money.

Now that Chandler and Joey have been winning several blocks in a row, more and more miners are joining, all with their own ASIC mining machines. This is good as it adds a higher energy fence for bad actors to climb. But with so much mining power, contests are beginning to get solved too quickly.

If blocks complete too quickly, Bitcoin's pre-determined release schedule will inflate. Even though there can never be more than 21 million Bitcoin total, users want to avoid 50,000 Bitcoin dumped into circulation one day because miners win contests every 10 seconds rather than 10 minutes.

Satoshi added his unique invention to combat this problem, *the difficulty adjustment*. This was the missing piece of the puzzle that plagued every version of electronic money before Bitcoin.

The difficulty adjustment is a software protocol that makes the contest easier when there is less mining power (typically fewer miners). It makes it more difficult when there is more mining power (typically more miners) such that each block is completed on average every 10 minutes over time.

Technically, the difficulty adjustment occurs every 2,016 blocks (about every 2 weeks). For illustration, if, over a two-week period, blocks are solved every 5 minutes, then the next two weeks would adjust the difficulty such that they take 15 minutes. It would average out that 4-week period to 10-minute blocks.

This adjustment is made by extending or shrinking that proof of number range. As more miners (or more mining power) join the network, that original proof of work range for the 500-sided dice might shrink to "less than 3."

In this case, every miner rolling a 500-sided dice must hit a 1 or a 2. It makes it much more difficult, twice as hard, with only a 0.4% chance of rolling 2 numbers out of 500 possibilities. But since more ASICs are running, this helps lengthen the contest's duration closer to its 10-minute target.

Conversely, if many miners leave, turn off, or use less computing power, this range will expand. The proof of work number might be any number under 25. It would help the people like Ross and his pet monkey, who only have one dice to roll (very little hash power). And rolling anything from a 1 to a 24 is much easier on a 500-sided dice.

With the mounting costs of computers and electricity, miners will eventually turn off if they can't win enough contests. We've seen this repeatedly happen, whether small-time operators or entire sovereign nations, like China, initiate a regional mining ban.

When this happens, it continues to re-distribute mining power globally. Game theory motivates others to join when there's an opportunity. If hash power decreases and miners leave, new ones will join. And as Bitcoin's price rises over time, even the rare chance of obtaining a fraction of a Bitcoin becomes valuable.

You'll recall that mining contests that started in 2009 issued 50 Bitcoin per block every 10 minutes. But at only 10 cents per block, that equated to a minuscule reward of only $5 per block. Yet any miner holding those 50 Bitcoin today is probably quite happy.

The Bitcoin protocol prevents anyone, anywhere in the world, from bypassing the computational integrity of proof of work. Regardless of any ulterior motive, one can only guess the correct input or not. This way, everyone agrees on a single source of truth in a decentralized system. No one can corrupt consensus. The governor of Bitcoin is math, not humans.

For the soldiers attacking Byzantine, proof of work removes the need for an arbitrary time to attack the castle. That was always the problem. What if a spy told one of the generals to attack at 2 pm instead of 4 pm? That would foil the whole plan.

Bitcoin's consensus mechanism creates its own clock without minutes or seconds. It becomes a clock of value. Soldiers know when to attack Byzantine because of an entirely different set of rules formed by proof of work, rather than trusting what someone tells them.

Money has never had a clock of value because fiat isn't fixed to anything, as it once was to gold. Fiat is created out of thin air, so there's no tie to real-world measurements, like a clock.

When you make $100 an hour, that money you receive ties to the one hour of work you performed in the physical world. But a central bank's printing of $100 is separate from actual work.

You work off a clock with 24 hours, while the Fed works with one with 30 or 50 hours. Their hours keep growing, which devalues your hours. More hours on a clock make each hour less valuable.

You can't make a clock tick faster or add more numbers to a clock. It is a closed system. This allows the entire world to coordinate off one standard. If you're meeting someone at 2:30 or going to be 15 minutes late, people know what that means.

Bitcoin is a clock for money. You can never add more Bitcoin, and you can't change the issuance rate due to the difficulty adjustment. People can plan and budget based on a strict schedule and rules. Like a clock, Bitcoin is a closed system. 1 Bitcoin will always equal 1 Bitcoin.

Fiat money devalues our proof of work. It distorts our personal clock of value. That $100 you took an hour to earn becomes 2 hours in hindsight due to inflation. And soon after 3 hours. You end up having less ownership of the monetary network by doing nothing but holding your money.

Bitcoin could also be printed out of thin air if it were available for anyone to right-click and duplicate. After all, Bitcoin is purely digital. The digital world must tie to the physical world. There has to be a fixed representation on each side of the portal from the analog world to the digital world.

This is the genius of mining as a method to bring Bitcoin tokens into the Bitcoin economy. Mining incurs real-world energy, expenses, and time. From those real-world events, it creates a digital representation in the form of the Bitcoin token.

Energy gets transferred from its value as electricity to its value as money. It's why Satoshi originally called Bitcoin *electronic cash*. It represents the electricity expended to create Bitcoin.

A person's clock of value transmits from the physical world into the digital world. There's no loss of signal. It retains its integrity. This real-world necessity for its creation prevents Bitcoin from being counterfeited or printed.

Ironically, greed motivates honesty and fairness when people have different backgrounds, beliefs, and ethics. Greed is something all humans have in common whether they agree with each other, are politically left or right, good or bad, rich or poor, purple or brown, God-fearing or atheist.

Even a monk or priest is motivated by money for its utility. It's why they seek donations. They want money for what it can do for them or their community.

Equally, criminals want money. If they could make money and not rob a bank or kidnap people, they would. But for lack of options or resources, they resort to crime.

Satoshi created a system that anyone can use to earn and secure money. Regardless of what their motivation is, the result is accounting. Everyone's preferences and morals get funneled into accuracy and security, all because they can grow their wealth. This encourages more users to join, making the ledger more secure and decentralized.

Meanwhile, our original friends in New York are seemingly living the good life. Monica, Rachel, and Phoebe continue happily contributing to the network as nodes. And as Bitcoin's price increases, they see their wealth increase.

Ross has given his pet monkey a break and simply enjoys Bitcoin as a payment system. He earns, saves, and spends entirely in Bitcoin. With apps, debit, and credit cards, no one even has to know but him.

Chandler and Joey, however, hear from critics and the media how damaging and destructive Bitcoin mining is to the environment. It uses way too much energy. So they sell their ASICs and even their Bitcoin. They're out. They can't be a part of something so pollutive and damaging to the world.

14

PROOF OF ENERGY

"Well-informed people know that it is impossible to transmit the human voice over wires as may be done with dots and dashes of Morse code, and that, were it possible to do so, the thing would be of no practical value."

Boston Newspaper, 1865

M ost critics of Bitcoin mining and its energy usage have their hearts in the right place but have misplaced their heads. They see a new technology that consumes a lot of energy. But since they don't understand Bitcoin, it's "bad" for the environment.

Why spend energy on something that isn't necessary and one that reportedly uses as much energy as a small country?

Without an appreciation for the problem Bitcoin solves, Bitcoin Mining's proof of work mechanism will always seem like a waste of energy.

How can we place a value on the energy someone chooses to pay for and use in their life? What is good or bad energy?

Government-inflated currencies can't be criticized because there's no easily measurable relationship to energy. Like a hair dryer, Bitcoin Mining is completely transparent in its energy usage, so it's easy to criticize when it's measurable.

In 2017, the mainstream media propagated articles on most news platforms touting that Bitcoin mining would consume all of the world's energy by 2020. But every year since this statement was made, Bitcoin mining has consumed less than 0.1% of global energy consumption. 1/10th of 1% of the energy consumed by the entire planet goes to Bitcoin mining.

To put this into perspective, if $100 represents all of the global energy in the world, 1 penny of that goes to Bitcoin mining. And actually, it's a fraction of a penny.

The world uses just over 175,000 TWh (terawatt-hours) per year. Bitcoin mining's annualized energy consumption has hovered around 100 TWh, which is 0.05% of the entire global energy consumption. But accounting for peaks, which have reached as high as 150 TWh, that is still less than only 0.08%.

Indeed, this is as much energy as an entire country uses. But only when you cherry-pick a tiny country like Austria that has 1/5th the population of California. Austria and Bitcoin Mining's total energy consumption combined is less than Christmas Lights or Facebook, separately.

Bitcoin mining's 0.1% usage is considered technically and statistically insignificant. It's an acceptable deviation from zero. Furthermore, 60% of this 0.1% energy usage comes from wasted, stranded, or otherwise off-grid resources unavailable, inaccessible, or discarded by others.

Bitcoin mining takes no energy available for anyone else because miners can't afford it. Retail electricity costs are too expensive, not knowing how long a miner will lose contests before finally winning a reward. And that's if it's ever won.

Like many aspects of Bitcoin, its protocol is incentivized by a moral code and enforced by math. This code says, "you must find the cheapest energy possible, or you won't profit."

On top of its tiny energy usage, Bitcoin mining doesn't emit any CO2 (carbon dioxide) or other greenhouse gasses or pollutive toxins of any kind. None.

The world emits over 35 billion metric tons of CO2 every year, yet Bitcoin Mining's contribution is warm air, which, in turn, is a utility for numerous other applications.

Much like a space heater, Bitcoin mining's only byproduct is heat. The only difference is a Bitcoin miner also secures the integrity of a fair, global monetary network free from state discretion and manipulation.

The components of an ASIC miner are similar to an external hard drive. They consist of computer chips, metals, plastics, rubber, etc. So we must account for the manufacturing of these parts. This gives the hardware of ASICs an annual carbon footprint of about 0.04% of all carbon emissions in the world. This percentage is so statistically small it rounds down to zero on any graph.

All of the above has been confirmed and published by the Environmental Protection Agency (EPA), several peer-reviewed University of Cambridge studies, and even a White House report touting the benefits Bitcoin mining has on the environment.

In fact, there are no academic or industry studies refuting these figures. There is simply click-bait politically sponsored media that spreads misinformation utterly devoid of facts.

Billionaire and co-founder of Ripple (XRP, a centralized altcoin), Chris Larsen, gave Greenpeace $5 million to spread information online about Bitcoin's damaging effects on the environment. After an assault across all social media platforms, it completely backfired due to facts, studies, data, and a misunderstanding of how Bitcoin mining interacts with energy.

Greenpeace went silent after ESG experts, climate scientists, and environmentalists (some ex-Greenpeace supporters) laid out the mechanics of Bitcoin mining. Had Greenpeace done its homework, it would have learned that mining is one of the best tools we have to clean up the environment.

The facts are that Bitcoin mining eliminates methane at the source like landfills and farms, making it a carbon-negative process. It arrests CO_2 from flared oil wells and other byproduct waste. And it builds out new distribution by partnering with renewable companies to bring energy to billions who have none.

If critics still think Bitcoin mining is wasteful given the facts, along with its value proposition to the world's underprivileged, they might want to take a look at their own relationship with energy.

I suspect critics of Bitcoin use tumble dryers, enjoy a warm house, log onto Google, and make toast. If hair dryers or tea kettles simultaneously mined Bitcoin, they, too, would be attacked for wasting energy.

When email first came on the scene, the U.S. Postal Service said it was too energy intensive and that their own physical carrier service was much more efficient and practical. Critics who are too early are often wrong.

Energy is the sole factor in every advancement, innovation, and modernization of civilization. The difference between prehistoric times and today is nothing more than humans' ability to harness and leverage energy from fossil fuels for human flourishing.

Our world's resources are only limited by what we can dream, conceptualize, dig up, repurpose, mold, combine, build, sell, and service. The spoils will always go to those who can harness those best.

If everything created by fossil fuels were to disappear, we'd be sitting on rocks, naked, staring at the sky (without framed glasses).

Look around you right now. Try to find something that isn't made of plastic, rubber, metal, or synthetic in some form. Or try to find something that didn't come from a factory, processed by a machine, or painted.

You are currently reading (or listening) to these words with technology, even if it's paper (and especially if it's paper) that exists due to fossil fuels.

Humans desire machines. Machines have improved our lives, from farming to manufacturing to transportation to data centers. All machines derive from fossil fuels. Everything we know and do is a product of finding ways to generate and consume more energy, not less.

Societies who reduce energy consumption don't prosper. And not coincidentally, a country's GDP directly correlates to its fossil fuel usage.

Disruptive and innovative technologies require more energy. In the same way that electricity uses more energy than candles, cars use more than horses, or computers more than typewriters, we need energy to bloom. Flowers bloom from CO_2, quite literally. CO_2 can only come from energy.

People want irrigation, plumbing, safe buildings, and bridges made from steel. Steel is also a technology that didn't seem necessary at first. Those in the wood and timber industry ran campaigns against steel because it required a lot of energy.

Bitcoin mining consumes 1/26th the amount of energy as steel. Steel allows us to build anything stronger, taller, and faster, replacing many older technologies.

Research and development require ample energy. Most of that never transforms into anything. But we encourage it because we know the benefit outweighs the cost.

Zoom now displaces thousands of executives flying and driving on roads to brick-and-mortar buildings because they can flip on their computers. What is the aggregate savings in energy consumption when you add up all that human travel expenditure?

Like money, energy is good. It's a tool. As early as caveman times, when we discovered fire, we deemed it "good." It allowed us to keep warm through the night, cook food, and transform things with heat. But wood is a biofuel. It requires removing a tree, burning it, and releasing carbon monoxide and organic compounds into the air.

We try to burn less wood due to these facts. However, we still find fire useful. We don't ban fire or say fire consumes too much energy. There's a trade-off between discoveries and the improvement of civilization.

The 17th and 18th centuries required killing whales to make the best candles, oils, and lubricants. It was primarily responsible for putting the sperm whale on the endangered species list. When electricity arrived, it was deemed a complete waste when we could just kill whales instead.

If we want to start placing value on what energy is wasteful or not, do we need to watch 20 seasons of The Kardashians? At what point are TV shows criticized for damaging the climate due to the sheer human and mechanical power required to launch and produce them?

What about the food we eat, the trucks, tractors, plows, and agricultural machines that harvest it for us? What about the buildout of security and safety we live in with ambulances, fire trucks, police, fences, locks, and cameras? Are they worth the generation of energy required to maintain them 24/7?

Airplanes use over 30 times the amount of energy as Bitcoin. And the aluminum needed for them to fly uses 39 times more energy to mine. But for some of us, the trade-off to arrive somewhere faster than riding a bike or paddling a canoe for 7 months straight is worth our hard-earned money.

This convenience and conservation of human effort are delegated to technology. Technology is 100% related to the capture and combustion of fossil fuels. No technology has ever existed, or will ever exist, that doesn't require reliable energy and a lot more of it.

Always-on-devices account for over 12 times the energy usage of the Bitcoin network. Are automatic garage doors important? What about a charged phone or ready-to-go laptop?

Porn represents over 37% of the internet's usage. Like Meta or Microsoft, porn comes from data centers with large computers and processors eating up unfathomable amounts of energy 24/7/365. But I don't recall Senators or the Green Movement attempting to ban the internet.

Can't we go back to libraries and the printing press? Or is the efficiency worth the cost? Do we enjoy colorful pixels with sound? Do we find artificial intelligence worthwhile or enjoyable?

Emissions from just 8 retail banks equate to 80 times more energy usage than the Bitcoin network. Yes, 80 times! Bitcoin's network can literally and holistically replace the entire banking system one trillion times over, using no more energy and emitting no more emissions than it currently does.

No one would believe you if you told them 100 years ago that you could condense the world's information into a small box in your pocket. Yet we've done just that with the smartphone. Bitcoin does this for the entire financial industry and its tentacles. It moves it all into one box called a miner.

If conservationists truly and honestly want to cut down on waste, Bitcoin's banking feature alone wipes out the entire climate crisis. Think about the sheer number of buildings, real estate, and executives attributed to banking in every town of every city of every state. Now think global.

Tens of millions of people work in finance, banking, and fintech. Imagine the amount of human capital that could free up by moving to Bitcoin.

Bitcoin allows investors to be their own financial advisor, banker, attorney, broker, and military-grade security all rolled into one when the asset is Bitcoin. That's because it is as useful as cash, yet indestructible and censorship-proof property.

Due to technology, it's unnecessary to have this web of inefficiencies all over the world to simply store and transmit value. But the media, under the influence of the government, will perpetuate the need for banks so they can track and control our spending behavior.

Then there are banking-adjacent investments like gold, which Bitcoin can entirely replace. Gold mining requires a lot of water to excavate, and often in regions where water is scarce. Toxic chemicals like cyanide that kill off wildlife and destroy the ecosystem are necessary to extract gold from ore.

It takes 20 tons of dirt removal by large earth movers to excavate the amount of gold to make a single wedding ring.

Bitcoin doesn't remove or destroy any valuable or limited resources that any living creature needs to survive. A single Bitcoin transaction uses the same energy as a web search or Instagram post. Do we really need to see another filtered photo of food on a plate?

Everything from air-conditioning to forced heat, incubators to refrigerators enhance the quality of our lives, and every single one uses multitudes more energy and emits more CO_2 than Bitcoin.

Critics often think that energy is limited, and thus any energy user is bad if they, the critic, don't need it. But this logic fails to understand the principles of energy.

We get the entirety of the earth's energy from the sun. Period. The free, available sunlight is our planet's sole source of all available energy in any other form.

Hydrocarbons like oil, coal, and natural gas are secondary to the sun. These resources store the sun's energy from countless lifetimes ago, acting as nature's batteries.

Living organisms, animals, and plants absorb the sun. Over time lifeforms break down, sink into the soil, and decompose into organic matter. This decaying process forms the hydrocarbons - coal, oil, and gas. We colloquially call these fossil fuels because they're remnants from prehistoric times.

Once we bring fossil fuels to the surface and expose them to oxygen, they become highly flammable. We light them on fire to produce heat which produces steam.

This steam or pressure automatically turns a turbine. The turbine's axle has attached magnets that turn and spin across a coiled wire. This interaction creates electrons that zoom down the wire and to your home. We call this electricity.

As archaic as this process sounds, it's how we create electricity. If we can find a way, any way, to create friction between magnets and a coiled wire, we're good to go. The most common way to do this is by burning fossil fuels to produce pressure or steam to turn a turbine.

The end-user of electricity connected to a utility grid has nothing to do with the fuel source chosen by the energy producer. Whether hydrocarbons or renewables, it's up to the energy producer. Economics, regulation, customer mix, and location dictate the percentage of fuel sources they can use reliably.

Energy producers simply want to turn those turbines to create electricity for paying customers. They need to generate as much as someone can pay for it, but without generating more than is necessary, which is expensive and wasteful.

Over 80% of the resources used by energy producers around the world are fossil fuels. Fossil fuels are "limited' so we seek new areas to excavate. But similar to gold, they are only limited by whatever technology and investment we deem necessary to locate more.

You'll recall from high school biology that plants capture CO_2 from photosynthesis. When they die, they take that CO_2 and put it back into the ground. When we extract them as oil, coal, or gas and burn them, we release that stored CO_2 back into the air.

CO_2 creates a Swiss cheese ceiling above us, preventing the earth's heat from escaping. Just enough, however, seeps out through the holes. We need this ceiling to live. Without it, the planet would be inhabitable. It would be too cold without the CO_2 blanket. And without CO_2, we wouldn't have any greenery, which can only survive because of CO_2.

If too much CO_2 is present, however, temperatures rise. The deforestation of trees removes nature's governor of CO_2 (again, photosynthesis). So, in theory, we wouldn't have a rise in CO_2 with abundant trees and plants, or could prevent it from reaching dangerous levels.

We mainly use fossil fuels because they are highly dependable, efficient, inexpensive, and portable. As nature's batteries, we can bring energy wherever people choose to settle.

But let's assume for the sake of argument that it's better for the planet to reduce CO_2. It means we need to either burn fewer fossil fuels that cause CO_2 in the first place or figure out how to eliminate the CO_2 we generate from using hydrocarbons.

The extraction and conversion of oil into energy have numerous environmental impacts. It pollutes the air and water, destroys nearby habitats, and, of course, releases CO_2.

The buildout of the oil process is intensive on an ecosystem with new pipelines and drilling platforms. There are also accidental oil spills that have had devastating consequences on wildlife.

Coal is the dirtiest of fossil fuels. It releases over double the amount of CO_2 as oil per unit of energy. In addition to having the same damaging impact on the landscape as oil, coal mining releases harmful pollutants and toxins into the air, like cancerous sulfur dioxide.

Natural gas is considered the most efficient and cleanest of the three fossil fuels. But depending on its extraction method, it can also devastate the environment.

Roughly 66% of all natural gas extraction in the U.S. and Canada comes from fracking. This process injects sand and chemicals into the earth to break up (frack) rock formations and allow natural gas to escape to the surface. But this can lead to leakage of chemicals into water beds.

Where natural gas becomes worse than oil and coal is when it isn't burned (flared). When natural gas escapes from the ground, it releases in its raw form, methane. Methane is 84 times more warming and pollutive than CO_2!

Whereas CO_2 has that Swiss cheese ceiling to trap hot air, methane has 84 slices of cheese and without any holes. It is why we should burn gas and convert into CO_2 and not just vent aimlessly into the air as methane. This is the trade-off with natural gas.

Every time we turn on our gas stove, fire up our gas laundry dryer, or turn on our gas fireplace, there is a second or two where we release methane straight into the atmosphere for that brief moment until the gas combusts. Once it's burning, it releases the less warming greenhouse gas, CO_2. It's why environmentalists want us to electrify these household items.

Critics conflate energy and electricity. They forget that electricity is the product of fossil fuels in the first place. Renewables like solar, hydro, or wind make up only a small percentage of electricity available to consumers.

You can't say, "Electricity is good, and fossil fuels are bad," when the turbine that generates electricity turns because of a high concentration of fossil fuels.

Most agree that a shift toward renewable energy is good. If energy can come from sources that are less pollutive, then great. But these resources need to be reliable, accessible, and affordable.

Wind, hydro, and geothermal are abundant and natural. Wind can turn a turbine. Ditto for waterfalls, rivers, and creatable dams. Natural resources are already generating steam and pressure on their own, like bases of volcanoes, naturally occurring geysers, and hot springs.

All of these sources bypass the need for combustion, thus reducing the emission of additional CO_2. In that sense, we want more renewable energy.

But renewables are limiting due to numerous challenges. They aren't reliable, accessible, consistent, and in most cases, affordable. It's why we still rely mostly on an 80/20 mix of fossil fuels to renewables.

Here are 6 of the biggest problems with renewables that many aren't aware of:

1. Fossil fuels are necessary to create renewables. Steel, plastics, silicon, solar panels, insulation, and batteries all require fossil fuels to mine and produce those elements. Burning coal is necessary to make most solar parts.

There's no decent way to recycle all of the aging solar panels, many of which end their life cycle in 2030. Solar parts contain lead which is then dumped into our landfills, contaminating the soil and water beds.

We have to acknowledge that there's a cost for the greater good. Maybe the burning of fossil fuels is okay if it creates something that eventually is better for the environment.

2. The renewable shift has been one of optics and politics. Solar panels are largely produced in China due to the high manufacturing cost and the game we play with international ESG (Environmental, Social, Governance) scores.

Thus we delegate this dirty duty to build solar panels to China and increase our ESG scores. It is why China is the world's manufacturing plant. But then we point to China as a pollution offender.

Canada sits on a massive oil bed, with plenty to provide energy to the world. But due to their strong environmental and ESG policies, they have restricted most oil extraction within their borders. They, too, outsource this task to China.

Canada has incredibly friendly ESG scores. But Canada spends more energy importing oil on cargo ships from China. And you can guarantee that China's extraction process of fossil fuels is more pollutive than Canada's. China is one of the worst environmental offenders (just behind India).

Companies play the same shell game but with carbon credits. Apple likes to say it is a 100% renewable company, but they are far from it. The manufacturing of their components is very fossil fuel intensive. But because they have so much cash, they buy carbon credits from other companies with abundant clean energy.

It's as if I could eat unhealthy food but purchase the health food receipts of 10 other people and say, "See, I'm eating healthy." Carbon credits do nothing for the environment but shift responsibility.

3. Renewables have an intermittency problem. The sun doesn't always shine. The wind doesn't always blow. Rivers stop. Renewables are highly inconsistent as to when they provide energy and in what capacity.

A hospital that operates 24/7 needs an abundant (and redundant) amount of energy that can't rely on renewables. They can't afford even a 1-minute

interruption that could cause death because of failed incubators or defib-
rillators.

A steel plant can shut down for a couple of hours in an emergency, but
beyond that, the steel will harden. Without steel, forget about buildings
taller than three stories, railroads, trains, autos, bridges, freeways, ships,
appliances, and all industrial machinery and manufacturing.

Most industries can't accommodate inconsistent energy with blackouts or
curtailment. Even a basic refrigerator must be on 24/7 or food will spoil.

Data Centers run our connected information world. The internet and all
its cloud-based services, Google, Amazon, or even the Pentagon, require
millions of computers plugged in, computing with fans spinning every
second of the day.

Those photos, songs, videos, and documents you love to share across your
devices come from data farms with warehouses of computers. When it's
time to sit down and watch Netflix or check email, you know it's available.
Gamers, visual effects artists, and other computationally intensive work
requires constant electricity. This reliability comes primarily from reliable
fossil fuels.

Data centers don't emit any CO_2 emissions. Like Bitcoin miners, there's no
waste or pollutants outside of the manufacturing of the parts. Electricity
comes in. Computations go out. But up-time makes data centers valuable,
so they need uninterrupted electricity from the grid.

It might be another story if the earth's natural elements weren't sporadic.
Data centers would be happy to be 100% off-grid and relocate to the middle

of the desert with solar panels. But more is needed for consistent and redundant energy.

Only one "data center" of any kind can take this kind of unreliable energy, as demonstrated in the next chapter (hint: it starts with "Bit" and ends with "coin").

4. Building renewable infrastructure is crazy expensive. It requires institutional or venture capital level investment that doesn't return to investors for years, sometimes decades, and that's if they ever break even.

Connecting from an energy source to the grid costs roughly $2 million per mile of distribution. It may take billions to build an effective delivery system depending on location, distance, and reliability of renewable energy.

Someday batteries will be powerful enough to harness renewables. That will be a game-changer. It's the only way we currently know how to store electricity. But experts say we are multiple decades away from that technology. We physically can't compress enough electricity into a battery at scale or in a cost-effective way where it doesn't deplete or can transport.

Battery production is also pollutive and damaging to the environment, so we're back to the same problem as fossil fuel extraction. Batteries require excavating and processing raw materials such as lithium and cobalt, which need fossil fuels.

The optics of an electric car are environmentally friendly. You don't use gasoline which is a direct derivative of oil refinement. But the electrification of the car itself requires thousands of microchips per car and tons of fossil fuels, including all of the components, metals, tires, fabrics, plastics, etc.

A giant earth mover must move 250 tons of dirt to extract the materials to produce a single Tesla car battery. That tractor will burn 1,000 liters of fuel in the 12 hours it takes to move all that dirt.

The electricity that Tesla owners use rather than gasoline directly results from fossil fuels. That electricity comes from their local grid, which comes from a high concentration of fossil fuels, not renewables.

Let's acknowledge the facts. Fossil fuels give us the electricity that the most hard-core environmentalists want us to use. Therefore you can't say plugging your car into a socket is good, but plugging your Bitcoin miner in is bad. It's intellectually dishonest.

5. Renewables are location dependent. Next to intermittency, this is perhaps the biggest obstacle to mass adoption. If someone wants to avoid fossil fuels entirely, they must go off the grid, unconnected to any traditional electricity whatsoever. There's no other way to avoid the high concentration of fossil fuels that come from utility providers.

But living off the grid means you have to be right next to the renewable source and be flexible with its sporadic output. Energy users don't want to relocate to the source of energy. They want energy to come to them. This has always been the case and a challenge.

6. Electricity dissipates or slows down if it has to travel far distances. Historically civilizations have set up around seaports and waterways for commerce and trade. But those areas aren't typically where you find most energy sources. So power has always needed extensive infrastructure to deliver to populations.

Energy providers want to mix in as high a percentage of renewable energy as they can. They need renewables as a source to meet EPA compliance and state regulations. They are shut down if they don't reduce emissions from the burning of fossil fuels.

They also like the cheaper cost of renewables once the infrastructure is in place. But there again is the rub. Building out that pipeline from a renewable source to the grid is ridiculously expensive and in most cases, prohibitive.

Electrifying the world seems like a good idea. But how much electricity do we waste? Unlike water, electricity can't sit still in a bucket and wait for us to use it. By definition, electricity has to move. It is no longer electricity if it sits.

Behind your wall socket, even if you're not plugged in, your electricity is always flowing like a river. It's why we get shocked by loose or exposed wires. We can't simply turn electricity on or off. Instead we access it or not, similar to the internet.

Over 65% of our total available electricity is wasted and never used. It's lost in the transmission from the power plant, at the transformer level, and from inefficient appliances and items plugged in 24/7. There's a phantom drain on everything connected to electricity, on or not. It's the price we pay for convenience and immediacy.

If we electrify everything and a large percentage of that electricity is from fossil fuels, we are wasting more fossil fuels. The fossil fuels that make electricity also have their own loss in becoming electricity. 60% of coal and 40% of natural gas is lost during the process of electricity creation.

At least with natural gas, you can turn it off and conserve. It can sit still in a pipe or container. It's why gas tumble dryers and gas stoves are much more efficient than their electric counterparts.

Energy providers must account for peak demand and assume that "any day" could be when everyone wants to blow dry their hair, run their dishwasher, microwave their popcorn, and vacuum the house. The river of electrons sent to us must be ample enough to assume that on any one day, we might decide to throw an igloo party and blast the AC.

The fix is to address how energy producers turn those turbines in the first place and then how to reduce greenhouse gasses. Attacking consumers who want to pay for and use electricity for whatever they choose to do with that electricity is a little tyrannical and duplicitous.

Environmentalists who want to tackle climate change are wasting their time attacking a newer technology like Bitcoin.

15
PROOF OF MINING

"X-rays will prove to be a hoax."

Lord Kelvin, President of the Royal Society, 1883

At the time of publication, 30 Bitcoin mining companies are using 90 to 100% clean energy. Another 12 are completely carbon-negative, officially becoming gas mitigators.

All Bitcoin miners will eventually be carbon-negative (most likely by the time you read this book), as you'll see why and how below. It turns out, once again, it's just math.

Bitcoin mining isn't cheap. The ASICS can cost anywhere from $2,000 to $5,000 for one machine depending on how new or fast it is. Many people plug in ASICS that are 6 to 7 years old to lower their start-up costs. But beyond the cost of the machine, 90% of the mining costs are electricity.

Thus miners' only lever to be successful (profitable) is lowering or eliminating electricity costs. They have no control over the market price of Bitcoin and, therefore, the revenue they generate when they sell their Bitcoin block rewards into the Bitcoin economy (and that's if they win).

Remember, the mining rewards from the won contests continue to reduce by half every 4 years. In this way, the network incentivizes miners to find cheaper and cheaper energy. The only possible way is to take it when and where no one else wants it. That usually means it's unreliable, inconsistent, wasted, stranded, or otherwise useless to any other consumer.

Miners typically form a pool or raise funds to buy the ASICS, plop them into a storage container, like a mini data center, and hook them up to electricity and an internet connection. That's all that is needed. It's as simple as it sounds.

Due to this compact set-up (think the size of a storage shed or horse trailer, depending on scale), miners can land anywhere in the world. Nothing needs to be fast or efficient, including the electricity source. The mining machine itself is the only thing that needs to be quick to compete in the contests to find that proof of work number and win Bitcoin.

No Bitcoin miner anywhere in the world today can profit meaningfully by connecting to a traditional utility grid and paying retail electricity rates. Most past criticism of bitcoin mining has stemmed from this faulty assumption.

Mining is only profitable at scale using the most wasted, dirty, and orphaned energy sources. There is no other electricity cheap enough for miners to profit.

Imagine a donut shop where donuts represent "energy." All customers come in and buy donuts.

The shop attempts to stay in business by having donuts for everyone but doesn't want to overproduce and throw too many away at the end of the day. That's costly with labor, ingredients, and wear and tear on the mixing machines and fryers. They also can't afford to lose customers when demand is high.

A bitcoin miner makes a deal with the donut shop. The miner agrees to buy every donut at an extreme (and sometimes free) discount.

To obtain this insane deal, the miner shows up at the end of every day to buy any donuts that weren't sold and are about to be dumped in the trash. The miner will buy all of them if too many were made, or they ended up deformed, broken, cold or fallen on the ground.

On days when suddenly everyone is craving a donut, the miner won't come into the store. They'll sit tight until the donut shop tells them there are more stale and crumbled donuts to pick up. Miners are unique because they don't have to eat donuts daily. It does not affect their diet.

In this way, a bitcoin miner balances out the donut shop's business. The donut maker can concentrate on making the best donuts in the most efficient way possible. A miner will buy if there is an excess but also sit tight when higher-paying customers are available.

Here's where it gets better:

The donut shop wants to expand. It wants to enter a new town where people have yet to access donuts. The miner will follow and become the first customer.

The miner will buy every single donut (again at an extreme discount) until the town's customers begin to discover donuts and pay retail rates. Then the miner backs off. Rinse and repeat.

This is the arrangement bitcoin miners make with every significant energy and oil company in the world. It's a win-win for both.

Since Bitcoin is location agnostic, it can go straight to wind-intensive regions in coastal areas, solar in barren plains, hydro in remote jungles, geothermal in the middle of oceans, or at the base of volcanoes. Cold or hot, livable or not.

Miners go to equators, dams, rivers, landfills, farms, distilleries, oil refineries, etc. These places are natural, existing, and kicking off energy or waste. Bitcoin miners will convert all of it into electricity to run their machines.

If miners don't show up, all that energy goes to waste. No one else wants it or can access these remote places. It brings a consumer (the miner) to the energy source rather than the other way around. Bitcoin mining is the first industry ever to be able to do this.

Now infrastructure, prosperity, and an economy can expand from desolate areas where people lack electricity or running water, or schools. This is already happening in many places. Africa is one example.

Africa's continent is filled with abundant, renewable sources. But 600 million people, 40% of Africa's population, have no electricity. Miners co-locate to these remote areas to help build and provide free or cheap electricity from hydro sources. Miners can immediately harness these renewables and subsidize the build-out of a grid to populations and, in turn, get cheap electricity for themselves.

As a customer of first resort, miners provide the revenue renewable companies need to construct their distribution system. A renewable provider's goal is to connect to the grid. And the energy producers will happily take renewable energy if there's a distribution system to reach them.

Miners come in as anchor tenants and bridge the financing gap until there's transmission infrastructure. It incentivizes the build-out of more solar, wind, and hydro renewables while providing immediate cash flow for investors since miners begin buying on day one. And as energy grows, so does the area along the distribution line.

As a customer of last resort, miners can then turn off when higher paying customers finally arrive with a grid connection. This flexible energy usage by bitcoin miners helps fill the valleys while allowing the energy provider to enjoy the peaks.

Miners act as a balancing mechanism to the intermittency issues renewables have. Since renewables depend on mother nature, their energy generation doesn't coincide with energy consumption. This is the biggest problem that grids face: imbalance.

Miners will take solar during the middle of the day when it's overly abundant, and most of it goes to waste. There's too much. And when solar is off at night, miners can shut down to allow enough capacity for other customers to stream Netflix and run their laundry.

The energy source doesn't matter. Whether wind, hydro, or geothermal, this clean energy gets dumped into the ground or lost because it's generated at the wrong time or place. But miners can turn off and on and go anywhere, anytime, 24/7.

This shape-shifting flexibility helps stabilize the grid. Bitcoin miners are the perfect customer to balance it out. They take excess energy at a discount and turn off when the energy providers can sell at a higher price to someone else. All of this gets negotiated into a contract for miners to have the cheapest electricity possible so they can profit.

One of the most apparent reasons grids can't rely on renewables is this instability. Matching supply and demand is one of their trickiest feats with the mixture of renewables. It's why we still predominantly use fossil fuels, as there is no guesswork.

But when a customer like a bitcoin miner comes into the mix, it helps solve the unpredictability of mother nature, much like the analogy of the donut shop operator.

Large data centers and tech companies, like Amazon or Google, are centralized. They can't shut down to curtail electricity usage when the grid is strained. What they gain in complete control over their users, they lose in flexibility with energy consumption and conservation.

Bitcoin miners are mini data centers but decentralized and spread out over thousands of locations worldwide rather than one central warehouse.

Each of the millions of mining machines separately runs the entire bitcoin ledger and competes for block rewards. As long as one of the miners is mining, the network continues block after block, 10 minutes at a time.

Whereas Microsoft or Apple requires all their data servers to run 24/7, it only takes one $2,000 ASIC miner to mine the entire Bitcoin blockchain. So any miner can turn off, stay off, and then turn back on. It doesn't affect

Bitcoin's network. But if some Twitter servers turn off, some customers will lose access.

In addition to consuming any available renewable energy anytime and anywhere, Bitcoin miners also make energy out of waste from other industries. The conversion of this waste prevents greenhouse gasses from entering the atmosphere, turning Bitcoin mining into a carbon-negative process.

30% of oil producers have a gas pipeline or distribution system to sell the gas as part of their business model. This is good. It's captured and used as energy. The other 70%, however, are solely drilling for oil and have no way to transport or store the gas. The gas gets in their way. So it goes wasted.

Oil producers must flare off (burn) this gas to prevent methane escaping. This too is good. However, the flaring creates CO_2.

Bitcoin miners prevent this CO_2 from entering the atmosphere in the first place by placing their mining rigs on site with the oil producer. The miner captures the gas before it's flared as CO_2. They divert the methane gas directly into their own generator to turn a turbine to create electricity to run their mining equipment.

Almost every major energy company globally collaborates and co-locates with miners to meet regional regulations, state flaring limits, and increase their ESG scores. It gives energy generators tax incentives while giving the miners cheap, wasted, and stranded energy that would otherwise produce CO_2.

But CO_2 is only part of the problem. Of greater concern is when the gas isn't flared and instead just vented into the atmosphere as methane.

Remember, methane is 84 times more warming than CO_2. It's absolutely the worst byproduct of gas.

Many oil wells and sites either go bankrupt or shut down. These orphaned wells still emit methane since there's no flare to burn it off. Flaring is expensive for companies as is, so when they've abandoned a site, they cease operations. It is a huge environmental problem as no one is babysitting these sites.

There are an estimated 29 million wells globally that have been abandoned. Miners now move to these dead sites and combust the methane fumes to run their rigs. This captures the methane and converts it into electricity for miners.

The wasted energy from these dead sites alone can power the entire Bitcoin network 10 times over. It's one of the cleanest ways Bitcoin miners can help reduce greenhouse gasses.

Who would be against someone willing to come in and solve the leaking methane from abandoned oil wells? Not environmentalists if they understood how this works.

It's like someone invented a magical device and gave it to us to combat climate pollution. It stabilizes grids, subsidizes renewables and new build-outs, and removes greenhouse gasses from other industries. Meanwhile, it secures a transparent accounting ledger. But because this magical device is called "Bitcoin," it is considered evil and damaging to the environment.

Oil drilling emits about 40% of all methane emissions due to flaring or abandoned sites. Another 30% comes from landfills and the other 30% from agricultural farms.

Methane is the real enemy, not CO2. Yes, we want to reduce CO2. But if CO2 is theoretically driving a car at 1 mile per hour toward a cliff, then methane is moving at 84 miles per hour toward the same cliff. Which car should we focus on first?

Let's go after methane with a vengeance. In conjunction with NASA, the United Nations Environmental Program has said that reducing methane is the best chance we have at significantly reducing climate change. It's the most robust lever we have as humans to do something rather than talk about it.

Many need to realize just how much methane we emit due to our over-consumption of junk that ends up in the city dump. We produce over 4.5 trillion pounds of trash each year. Oil producers and landfills account for over 70% of all methane emissions. Bitcoin mining can entirely negate this.

There are almost 3,000 active landfills just in the U.S. 30% of these sites have spent millions to flare off the methane with nicely decorated smoke stacks and green parks above ground. Some people may not even know they are near a landfill due to architecture or other visual cover-ups like dog runs. The dumps that are near populations can convert the methane into natural gas and pipe it to energy providers. It works as it should.

But the other 70% of landfills are in remote areas, nowhere near populations, so they can't sell the gas. Thus there's no reason to spend millions on a distribution system. Even if you have investors, getting the proper permits and meeting regulations takes up to 4 years.

These landfills sit in the open air emitting methane 24/7. No caps, no flares, just vented straight into the atmosphere. These dumps are "Super-emitters" since there's no incentive, no financing, and no system to encourage methane capture.

But once again, in exchange for ridiculously cheap or free electricity, Bitcoin miners will happily plop a single container on-site, right on the landfill, hook up about 50 ASICs or so, and connect them to a generator that runs off the combusted methane that converts to electricity.

Most landfills are regulated by municipalities that have to spend hundreds of thousands a year. So cities are ecstatic to eliminate this expense when miners can deal with their methane problem. No grid connection or pipeline build-out is needed - no permits, no waiting, nothing. Landfill operators simply have to open their doors and say okay set your miners down and start eating methane.

Running just one of these containers with about 40 ASICS for one year will reduce so much methane that it has the same effect on the planet as planting 5 million trees and letting them clean CO_2 out of the air for the next 10 years.

But Bitcoin miners aren't running for only one year, and they're not landing on just one landfill. They'll run forever and take every dump if offered.

Once landfills are at trash capacity and no longer functioning, they continue to emit methane for the next 15 years. Here in the U.S., we have an additional 10,000 landfills that are full but still emitting methane. They emit the equivalent of 20,000 metric tons of CO_2 per year, or the equivalent of gas-powered cars driving 50 million miles.

The other 30% of methane comes from farms and wastewater. These places with dairy and pig farming, even alcohol distilleries, can all benefit in the same way as oil producers and landfill operators can. Everyone wins. And the climate thanks them for it.

No other energy consumer can do this. No other industry of any kind is willing to go directly on-site to a dump and convert that methane into electricity. Other businesses are location-dependent, require too large a footprint, or need a distribution system. Not Bitcoin miners. They are the raccoons of consumption. Give them a trash can anywhere, and they'll find all the energy they need.

Bitcoin miners can heat entire houses, hotels, fisheries, and swimming pools. They can dry fruits, timber, coffee beans, vegetables, and marijuana houses. They can even create drinking water for communities through desalination. They heat dirty water and condense the steam back into clean water.

A newer technology called OTEC (Ocean Thermal Energy Conversion) is now harnessing the temperature differences in the ocean to mine Bitcoin and provide clean electricity to populations. It's perhaps the largest un-tapped energy source our planet offers.

Bitcoin miners plop floating rigs in the middle of the ocean to take advantage of the deep cold water. The water is pumped up to interact with the heat from the Bitcoin miner.

These temperature differences create energy to turn a turbine and produce electricity. The electricity is then transported back from the floating miner to land via a cable that can provide electricity for up to a billion people who don't have access to, or can't afford, electricity.

Mining is eating up cooking oil and sewage, using both sources as fuel. It's cleaning up dirty lakes in Guatemala. It's providing electricity to people in the Congo, 90% of whom don't have electricity and must burn down trees for heat. This biofuel process is toxic and unhealthy.

When your money debases and your government's fiat keeps you poor, the environment is the last thing you care about.

One reason El Salvador was the first country to make Bitcoin legal tender is due to their abundant source of geothermal energy. Volcanoes boil and scorch the water underground creating steam that can be captured to turn turbines and generate electricity.

El Salvador is creating an entire "Bitcoin City" on this premise with mining and "Bitcoin Bonds" that finance the build-out while giving investors Bitcoin.

Bitcoin becomes guaranteed money for a developing country otherwise oppressed and disadvantaged against a fiat system of debt owed in U.S. dollars to the IMF and World Bank. Since El Salvador can't print U.S. dollars to pay back their debt as we can, they'll make their own money with Bitcoin and their country's natural resources. In the process, this helps the environment by incentivizing capturing waste to convert into energy.

PRTI (Product Recovery Technology Intl.) boils wasted tires back into their original fossil fuels. With over a billion unused tires per year, most are buried or burned, neither of which are environmentally friendly. But with a new patented process, PRTI captures all of the natural gas from the tire-boiling process to generate electricity to mine Bitcoin.

Imagine a future where all these underprivileged areas of the world with no other way out of poverty can suddenly tap into their natural resources. A single turbine under a waterfall in Zimbabwe, Brazil, or Argentina can bring prosperity and human decency to citizens. This can then extend to schools, hospitals, roads, and housing.

Bitcoin mining can monetize almost any remote area of the world where there is natural motion of some kind.

Humans want to flourish. Energy is necessary for that. Bitcoin mining can make it cheap, free, and even profitable to add more energy to live. It protects those who are most financially discriminated against and in need. It protects wealth and thus health.

If someone wants to solve the climate crisis, Bitcoin mining should be encouraged - everywhere. And not just for its greenhouse gas mitigation but for the security of a monetary network that all countries and people who are the worst environmental offenders could benefit from.

Fix their money, and you fix the need to destroy the planet to survive.

Fiat money is broken, so we work longer and harder (more energy) to utilize machines and products (more energy) to make money to replace our debased currency due to inflation (more energy). Fiat is the problem, not a Bitcoin mining machine that fixes this.

Energy providers will go out of business if electricity isn't available when their customers want it. And unless customers decide to unplug, go off-grid, and stop buying things, we'll always need an abundance of energy. Every single purchase of a good or service is a vote for more energy in the future.

There is a direct environmental cost to over-consumption. Our landfills run out of room. Our oceans fill with plastics. Our skies cloud with smog.

Regardless of your view of the environment, fossil fuels, or renewables, unnecessary consumption isn't helpful. But this is what an inflationary world creates.

Bitcoin mining fixes this by using 1/10th of 1% of the world's energy. Meanwhile, it will eat up the methane that others create and emit only heat in the process.

16

PROOF OF DEFLATION

"There's no chance that the iPhone is going to get any significant market share."

Steve Ballmer, CEO Microsoft, 2007

Anyone who wants to solve environmental or climate concerns wants to solve money. Fiat is the most significant contributor to energy waste, far more than any other industry or process.

Fiat's oxygen is inflation. The U.S. dollar thrives when its value is depleted over time because debt becomes less meaningful in the future. Even though the government's debt increases every year, inflation makes those payments less relevant.

If you buy a $500,000 house with a 5% mortgage, you pay $2,083 monthly interest. That payment represents 0.42% of the house's total market value. If inflation is 10%, then in one year, that house is now valued at $550,000.

It requires 10% more dollars to purchase the same house. But your fixed $2,083 monthly payment is now 0.38% of the asset.

Inflation has increased your asset value up 10% but not your debt payment. Thus, inflation encourages debt. It encourages leveraging and buying assets on credit.

Since fiat loses value over time, it incentivizes overspending. It's smarter to buy today than tomorrow with inflation.

Those with high debts, like the government, big corporations, Wall Street, banks, and the ultra-wealthy, will do everything to keep inflation going. They can borrow more, leverage more, pay less, and grow their wealth.

Inflation helps the rich get richer. But also the poor get poorer. The poor can't afford the assets to give them this advantage. However, the consumables that the poor depend on are now 10% more expensive with 10% inflation.

Much of the lower (and even middle) class doesn't have the collateral to obtain the plentiful cheap loans made from money printing. So while assets appreciate in monetary value, the goods and services of the poor rise in price. They spend their money to exist rather than to grow.

Depending on what side of this fence you're on, you might benefit from this if you own real estate or other appreciable assets on credit. However, removing this fence is possible so that everyone benefits rather than excludes access.

Fiat's asphyxiation is deflation. When there are fewer (or fixed) units in a money supply, it increases the value of each of those units as they have finite scarcity. This raises the relevance of debt payments as they become more meaningful over time.

Deflation discourages leverage, credit, and over-consumption. It encourages saving and investing. It motivates careful purchases that one can afford. Knowing any money we hold onto will become more valuable helps minimize lazy consumption.

A money supply doesn't need to reduce to be deflationary. It can be fixed and known. A healthy economy increases its GDP - its goods and services. It creates more available consumables to attract limited money. Prices then decline to compete for an abundance of goods.

Bitcoin is deflationary because of its fixed supply. Regardless of how much the government inflates fiat, Bitcoin can give all users the benefit of a deflationary economy. But they have to switch over.

Holistically, money supplies are not supposed to inflate. Money should not be manipulated with overly cheap credit, subsidies, and stimulus.

Those all sound positive to most of us as we've never known a monetary system that wasn't inflationary. But we also think short-term and forget about recessions, bubbles, higher prices, and taxes - all resulting from inflation.

Money works in a deflationary system because our past time is appreciated rather than distorted.

House prices, car prices, education costs, energy prices, etc., all come down with less money in circulation. Assets trend toward or return to their *utility value*.

Assets no longer have to be financialized in a deflationary economy. When investors can save because their money is worth more in the future, they don't have to purchase things they don't want, like a fourth or fifth house.

With deflation, there's less need to seek a premium to hurdle the inflation rate. Most haven't stopped to think about why they invest - to beat inflation. Prices rise, and investors want money to grow faster to buy more in the future.

But this process of chasing inflation causes those who need the utility of an asset to pay more. Investors monetize those assets. They don't really *need* them.

Those who need a house to live in have to pay a higher price because investors use them as piggy banks. Investors want the appreciation that will occur due to inflation.

If people can reliably and consistently make money flipping or investing in real estate, they should do it (I do it). We don't have a choice against inflation. And without options, you have to game the system to run faster to stay in place. Real estate is one of the oldest, best, and most well-known games for doing this.

Yet why is it that more and more families can't afford homes? Why does it require a larger percentage of income every year to acquire one?

Bitcoin fixes this. Bitcoin allows the capture of inflation and makes everything priced against it deflationary. It provides value for those seeking inflation protection without prohibiting others from an essential utility asset, like real estate.

If money is simply the storage of time, there should be a simple vault that isn't dependent on outside factors like squatters, vacancy rates, deterioration, and maintenance.

There should be a way to spend your stored time fractionally without displacing or revealing the rest of your wealth. There should be a way to transport your wealth privately and secure it forever.

If the utility value hasn't changed on an asset, like adding a second story to a house, then the value of the dollar has gone down against it. "Appreciation" is just another way of saying that the money supply has inflated, so it requires more units for the same utility.

That house that is now 30% more than last year either has 30% more utility in a free market, or the fiat money is worth 30% less because it inflated. Unless there's been a complete renovation or build, that house hasn't increased utility by 30%. It's the money supply that has increased by 30%.

No one really wants precious metals. Most don't really want income properties. Most don't want to invest in corporate or government bonds. They want the additional money those investments can get because things become more expensive.

We might like investments for what they say about us. They become a flex. They may signal to others that we are responsible or enterprising. But no one wants to become a landlord. Investors endure it because they want the money it potentially brings, similar to many careers and jobs.

There's the job we do and then the job we do to protect the job we do. This is the problem with inflation. It requires us to have two jobs rather than one.

The podiatrist who spent her life studying and honing her skills in medical school earns in fiat. She'd store her excess energy in a savings account but loses spending power to rising prices. Thus she's forced to find more risky ways to preserve her excess contribution to the economy.

The podiatrist can't let her money sit somewhere "safe." She needs to return that money to the topsy-turvy economy to earn more money to compete with inflation, hopefully. Her sacrifice to become a podiatrist is reduced when a debasing currency diminishes that energy.

She can be a pottery maker, a professor, or a plumber. It makes no difference. Those specialized skills produce more value than they can consume in a day. If saving that value goes down due to inflation, she must invest. Otherwise, it's a guaranteed losing proposition to simply hold fiat. So she might as well give it a shot.

But investing is itself a specialized skill. It takes years of college, finance degrees, and regulatory licenses. Even then, like a physician, it requires years of experience.

How is the plumber or pottery maker supposed to invest without taking on more risk than they already took to acquire their skills?

They could always pay someone like a financial advisor or broker to secure the work they've already done. But this requires them to burn off more of their valuable past work in the form of fees to secure the money in the first place. It is yet another form of inflation.

It's as if we're all standing outside a casino with our net worth. The longer we stand there, the more our money evaporates. So we enter the casino to play games to grow our money. But not everyone can afford the table limits. And not everyone is a professional gambler.

Inflation also sustains zombie companies that access newly printed money to buy back their shares. Common investors must spend more on the same stock to acquire the same benefit as those companies who received free money from cheap credit.

A company with inflated stock prices due to inflation didn't have to improve their systems, update a process, launch a new product, or gain new customers. They just took newly minted money in front of general stockholders. They pay nothing. Investors pay everything.

A healthy economy shouldn't prop up unsustainable companies or banks. Natural business cycles and business choices need to play out. It benefits the economy as it makes companies show their proof of work, become more streamlined, cut expenses, and seek value for customers.

Interest rates should be dictated by the free market, not by inflation. When borrowers are riskier, lenders charge more interest. When borrowers are more credit-worthy, lenders charge less interest. It's not rocket science.

That's how interest rates work when unencumbered by political and monetary influence. But inflation says, nope, let's just lower interest rates. Period. This distorts the health of companies that shouldn't be on life support.

Hundreds of banks and insurance companies received bailouts during the Global Financial Crisis of 2008 because they over-leveraged their lending at 35 to 1. Banks irresponsibly bundled mortgages into derivative products that were complete scams.

Those further from the money funnel lost their homes without the billions of dollars of handouts. They're the ones that paid for this excess.

We saw this happen again in March 2023 with Silvergate Bank and Silicon Valley Bank. Both regulated and federally FDIC-insured banks went under and into receivership when they couldn't liquidate fast enough to meet the demand of withdrawals. Both housed some of the largest VC, tech, and crypto companies in the world. However, the banks leveraged their deposits into long-term assets that they couldn't liquidate quickly enough once there was a bank run.

The math always balances out at some point. There is no free money. There is simply a redistribution of it - if not to someone else, then to our future self. This is the truth behind inflation's fake narrative that a little bit is healthy.

Then there are the honest businesses who succeed by their merit, not handouts. They are discounted by inflation's money manipulation. Small business owners have to focus more on competing with propped-up competition rather than spending time on innovation and improvement.

Public companies advance technology and spend money on research when it benefits their quarterly earnings and boosts their stocks. They're incentivized to improve and produce. But when money printing begins (inflation), there's less incentive to provide economic value.

Like when salt was money, people would spend time making salt rather than whatever they were trained and experienced to make.

Bitcoin's ultimate value is its agency for freedom. It allows individuals to pursue and communicate their interests. One can specialize in whatever one wants. One can then capture that value with Bitcoin. And because of Bitcoin's monetary properties, no other risk is necessary.

Bitcoin shifts the monetary premium away from investment assets and into itself. It improves the world by returning those assets toward their utility value.

The pottery maker, the professor, the plumber, and the podiatrist can store their excess energy contribution into Bitcoin rather than drive up the prices of other goods for those who can least afford them. Let Bitcoin increase in value rather than a house someone needs for shelter.

You can own a bunch of rare wine if you want to and find the best way to store and secure it. Or you can own Bitcoin. You can own Bitcoin instead of gold, buildings, commodities, artwork, or anything else that you wouldn't typically own if it were not for the hope of making money from it.

Setting aside hobbyists or enthusiasts, most will tell you all of the above is a hassle were it not for the potential profit. They all require maintenance, attention, security, insurance, and risk of human decisions.

Many of these things must also be custodied with someone else adding another layer or risk. Bitcoin is the only asset ever that makes self-custody safer and more secure than third-party custody.

Not everyone has access to financial products like pension funds. Only certain large companies offer 401k matching. Most people aren't connected to a trust or an endowment. And most need to have accredited investor status to gain access to appreciable assets.

But everyone has access to Bitcoin. It is the first and only asset in history available to everyone all over the world at any socioeconomic level. Bitcoin doesn't require that you meet income or net worth minimums. Why should those be requisites to secure and grow your money?

Because Bitcoin is a bearer asset with no counterparty risk, it offers complete, 100% ownership without risk of default or confiscation. The only requirement is to self-custody it so it isn't prone to company shenanigans.

Outside of that, there is no maintenance. You don't have to have a second job to buy and save Bitcoin. But like wine or artwork, if you enjoy Bitcoin as a hobby, you can spend as much time as you'd like on it without increasing the costs of housing or cars for someone who needs those.

Bitcoin's adoption shifts the monetary premium out of physical assets and into a digital one that takes no utility from anyone. Bitcoin appreciates as money. Period. Its value is money, not as a car to drive or food to eat.

Technology makes things cheaper. The whole point of invention, advancement, and creation is to make lives easier, more efficient, and more productive.

Technology gives us more time. It allows us to be in several places at once. And we can perform the work of 10 others with the right technology.

The amount of commodities we can harvest increases. We outsource labor costs to more efficient systems, robots, A.I., etc. It lowers the costs of businesses and, thus, the cost of commodities. Prices go down.

Whether it's a tractor replacing farm workers, the internet replacing a library, or software replacing accountants, technology brings down prices, labor, and the energy needed to accommodate that labor.

The core of energy conservation removes the energy expenditure of buying until necessary. Bitcoin reframes what consumption means for people. If you thread a sequence of events backward from a simple little purchase to its original creation, you'll discover a long line of energy expenditure.

There are the people who marketed and then stocked the product for you to find on the store shelf; the trucks which brought it to the distribution centers; the manufacturing plants outfitted with molds and robotic arms to make the product; the research and development to develop the product; along with the buildings, meetings, investment from venture capitalists, and the past energy it represents.

There are also the lawyers, accountants, and bankers who papered it all together. Add in the hundreds of employees driving to and from work, food, health benefits, etc., to get this one product.

The sequence is almost never-ending on the amount of energy it takes. And every time we make a purchase, we contribute to the continuation of this energy.

If the product adds value and enhances life, the energy moves in the right direction. We transfer the product's energy into our own generative energy to provide additional energy to the world.

But if a frivolous purchase ends up in a landfill, that energy breaks down into methane gas, which releases into the atmosphere as a noxious greenhouse gas.

Environmentalists who are intellectually honest and not swayed by politics favor deflation and, thus, Bitcoin without realizing it.

Deflation encourages people to be better stewards of the planet by incentivizing longer time horizons. Wealth can grow naturally without chasing risk-asset premiums with unnecessary energy on services and goods.

Every purchase becomes a thought experiment. Do I need this? How much Bitcoin will this cost? What will that Bitcoin be worth 4 years from now? If you can buy a new car for 1 Bitcoin today, will you regret knowing in 4 years, you could buy 3 cars with that same 1 Bitcoin?

People only spend their valuable Bitcoin on the best goods possible.

We teach our children to be smart and responsible with their money. But because of inflation's effects, we carelessly spend. Our children follow suit.

What used to be a consideration for something that was 20 bucks is now an afterthought. If you lose 20 bucks, you won't turn your house inside-out looking for it. The same can be said for 200 bucks today or 2,000 in a few years.

We live in a time when the entire world is aging, especially in the U.S., due to the baby boomer generation. As the population ages, demand decreases. Older people become more financially conservative and live off their assets and fixed incomes.

This reduced demand naturally reduces prices when not manipulated by inflation. Consumables adjust prices down to meet those expectations of demographics.

Ultimately, deflation allows consumers to get more for their money. And if not in quantity, at least in quality.

We will eventually price everything in Bitcoin. Maybe not officially here in the U.S., but any individual can begin doing this today. With a low-time preference, the Bitcoin standard makes everything deflationary over time.

When the iPhone 4 came out, it cost 2,857 Bitcoin. Then the iPhone 5 was released, and it cost 16.6 Bitcoin. The 6 was 2.17 Bitcoin. The 7 was 1.28 Bitcoin. The 8 was 0.24 Bitcoin. And so on and so on until the iPhone 13 was .02 Bitcoin.

The iPhone 14 rose to a price of .03 Bitcoin due to the global recession and credit crisis. But zooming out, deflation's impact moves in one direction only. This is in light of the iPhone inflating and costing more in fiat terms every year.

Our time is absolute and finite. The money that represents our time should also be absolute and finite. It is why Bitcoin is money. Fiat is not money. Fiat is time-theft.

Bitcoin isn't just software code. It's also a moral code. It is here to stop centralized authorities from stealing, inflating, and counterfeiting. All of this wastes energy and contributes to the problems governments say they care about. But they spend more money buying more bandages for a wound that can be prevented in the first place if they stop stabbing themselves with inflation.

Governments think Central Bank Digital Currencies (CBDCs) are the answer to this. Rather than combat inflation, they'll control the spending patterns of currency holders. Some good old-fashioned censorship and permission may solve the problem.

In China, where they already have their version of the digital yuan, a CBDC, they put expirations on the currency. Citizens must spend their money within a limited time frame, or it expires. This contributes to artificial GDP numbers, as expenditures become unnecessary consumption. You can't plan or save.

This monetary control keeps people at the mercy of the state. They want their citizens to work, comply, pay taxes, and be happy. With less opportunity and leisure, there's less ability to think, protest, and get in trouble.

The problem is that a CBDC only amplifies fiat's problem. As advocates would like you to believe, it doesn't get closer to Bitcoin's solution. Because a CBDC is programmable, a government will make it a social scorecard.

Didn't vote yet? Your CBDCs turn off. Spent too much on lotto tickets? They turn off. Tax returns, however, might be more manageable. The government knows exactly what you purchased with CBDCs and can adjust your stack on April 15th.

And just wait for the next pandemic. Governments will place distance restrictions on CBDCs to keep people in their zones. What better way to prevent a virus from spreading than not allowing commerce beyond specific neighborhoods.

Governments hate cash. Aside from physical printing, there's no record of who has it and how they spend it. Ironic that the government realizes everything is transparent on an open ledger, so they want one to spy on citizens.

Except with CBDCs, the ledger won't be open or decentralized at all. It will be hosted on their centralized server and manipulated to benefit them.

This is a breach nightmare waiting to happen. Almost every government agency and entity that you've ever known has been hacked at some point, and more than once. The data leaks alone will be pretty bad for everyone.

Bitcoin is the only system of value that has never been hacked.

Proof of work proves that Bitcoin is deflationary. With approximately 8 billion people worldwide, there is only enough Bitcoin for every individual to own 0.0026 Bitcoin. It is so scarce that each human being can only have 2.6 one-thousandths of a Bitcoin.

This demonstrates just how valuable accumulating Bitcoin can be. And how even small fractions can be worth fortunes in the future.

If you take the U.S. population of 330 million people and pretend that the other 194 countries aren't stacking Bitcoin, then there is still only 0.063 Bitcoin for every person.

Of the 21 million Bitcoin that will ever be available, there are already approximately 3.7 million that are lost forever. 1 million of those are the ones Satoshi essentially donated in the name of deflation. Those will never enter circulation. They will remain a tribute to Bitcoin's censorship-resistant properties forever.

Every hacker has tried to get their hands on Satoshi's 1 million Bitcoin. It just sits there on Bitcoin's blockchain for everyone to view. There's nothing to hide, yet no one can ever touch it.

What happens when adoption increases and people want to own 1 whole Bitcoin? With 3.7 million lost forever, only 17.3 million Bitcoin will ever be available. That means only .2% of the world can own an entire Bitcoin. Let that sink in, and plan accordingly as you think about Bitcoin's deflationary properties.

The other 2.7 million lost Bitcoin are from user error - lost hard drives, accidentally thrown away computers, lost keys, etc. Back when Bitcoin was worth only 1 penny, any user could easily plug their laptop into a wall socket and mine 500 Bitcoin. People were careless with them and needed to have a better security protocol.

Also, people died without realizing Bitcoin would ever be worth something in the future, so it died with the user. This is another deflationary property of Bitcoin. Passing with your Bitcoin becomes a selfless donation to all Bitcoin holders of the world. That amount of Bitcoin is taken out of circulation forever.

Of course, with careful steps, setting up a legacy system to pass your Bitcoin on to your family is important. This should be the goal of everyone with a multi-signature key set-up. But for those who have failed to do this, it becomes a charitable gift to the entire network.

Also, because Bitcoin's supply is fixed, most Bitcoin holders add value to the network simply by holding. By saving and not selling, they keep Bitcoin out of circulation, thus raising the value for those who need to transact with it. Their purchasing power rises as holders squeeze the supply for them.

Policymakers will always resist deflation. It scares them to death to see proof of work. They want a system where they can print away their debt even if the cost is the distortion of human action.

But citizens don't have to accept this. The 15,000 people geographically and physically able can stage an in-person, 60-day protest as they did with 2011's Occupy Wall Street.

Or, all 8 billion people on the planet can peacefully protest by saving in Bitcoin rather than fiat. No barricades. No arrests. No violence.

17

PROOF OF INFLATION

"Remote shopping, while entirely feasible, will flop... because women like to be able to change their minds."

Time Magazine, 1966

In traditional finance, we encounter interest rates in a sequence of events.

We begin our investment path with a savings account and want that rate as high as possible. We then acquire credit cards, buy a car, shop for a house with a mortgage, and want those rates as low as possible. Eventually, we buy stocks and bonds for our investment accounts and want those rates as high as possible.

Depending on what side of interest rates we sit, we want them to benefit us. But anything that has interest rates has risk.

There's the risk one takes as advertised in the interest rate and the hidden risk against the inflation rate. It's the latter that we need to pay attention to.

Interest rates are nothing more than the cost of time. Those who retain balances on credit cards are optimistic about the future value of their time.

An 18% rate on a credit card is similar to valuing your time at 18% higher one year from today. Otherwise, you wouldn't make that trade.

Investing rewards us for uncertainty. That's investing in a nutshell.

We gain a premium for delaying our spending power with the risk of losing it. Profit results from renting our excess resources to someone else and trusting they will return them. The interest rate reflects how realistic this level of trust is.

The problem is that inflation breaks this trust. It warps interest rates. We can't assess risk in real terms if we ignore inflation.

We accept that a $5 slice of pizza at our favorite pizza joint will, at some point, cost $6 on a subsequent visit. We'll still buy the slice. But we would question our sanity if a $5 bill morphed into 4 single dollar bills before our eyes. In both scenarios, we've lost 20% of our spending ability.

Inflation is hidden with more palpable and euphemistic brainwashing to sell it as healthy and natural. But inflation is not a natural function. It is 100% created and controlled by governments. It directly results from adding more currency into the supply, thus diluting its value.

The short-term effect of money injection only puts a bandage on an open wound that should be allowed to bleed and heal. The free market can't stabilize fairly or accurately when it is manipulated beyond utility value.

Like a helicopter parent that doesn't allow their child to skin their knee or learn the consequences of their actions, the government rewards bad behavior at the expense of those who are responsible.

Forgiving student loans is a noble and generous idea. But this is nothing more than money printing, which creates inflation for our future selves. It devalues the students who work two jobs, study to maintain their academic scholarships, and make sacrifices to pay for their education.

And what about the students who delay college altogether? What's the price of that missed opportunity?

During the C-19 pandemic, homeowners could freeze their rent or mortgage payments, some forgivable. How does it affect those who chose to continue paying what they agreed to or those who didn't buy a house because they were still saving? Only now, inflation is rising faster than their savings due to this same stimulus, so they're even further from their goal.

Loan forgiveness outsources to future tuition payments. Those will increase in the same amount as forgiven. Mortgage and rent forbearance plans become higher mortgage rates for new buyers and higher rents for others.

Businesses now have higher costs across the board due to trillions in stimulus. Everyone received more money. But it has to be paid back by someone.

Like a store that factors shoplifting into their prices, businesses delegate this cost to future customers. It's a game of musical chairs where someone is left standing without a seat at the money table.

If our money supply increases, we have little choice but to increase our personal money supply proportionally. We need to retain our percentage of the monetary network to avoid too much dilution.

You are diluted once when additional money enters the system. And you are diluted a second time if you don't receive your proportional share to everyone else.

Let's admit that inflation is a governmental mechanism that redistributes opportunity and wealth.

It took over 227 years to inject the first $6 trillion into the U.S.'s money supply. That is just an unfathomable amount of money. But it represents 227 years of growth, so we can accept it.

Right after C-19, we printed an additional $6.4 trillion in months. We compressed over two centuries of money issuance into a 2-month period. It is why inflation skyrocketed once the pandemic began to subside. The bills were due.

Of that $6.4 trillion, roughly $5 trillion (78%) went to the wealthiest. Granted, many of the wealthiest represent businesses and real estate that benefit others downstream. The hope is that it flows into smaller streams. But it rarely does, or at least in a fair way.

Inflation has been so rampant that we forget just how much a trillion dollars is.

If I stack $1 million in dollar bills on my desk, it will rise 43 inches tall. If I kept stacking until I had $1 billion, it would leave our atmosphere and reach over 67 miles into space.

And if I lived several thousands of lifetimes and could stack $1 trillion, the pile would extend 67,866 miles into space. For context, it would take stacking dollar bills from my desk to the international space station 267 times over to equate to $1 trillion.

Our $31.5 trillion national debt is roughly $95,000 per citizen or $250,000 per taxpayer (since some don't pay taxes). That's just federal debt. Add in the debt of all 50 states, private debt, and accounts payable (future debt like Medicare and pensions), and we have over $2.2 million in debt per taxpayer.

The average American doesn't make nearly that much money in their lifetime. How does that bill get paid?

We will pay this in the form of inflation. We'll pass it on to our grandkids. For them, a $40,000 car will cost $350,000, just as that $40,000 car was once $800 for our grandparents.

Every developed nation has this same problem. But many are 10 or even 100 times worse than us. Some have better debt-to-GDP ratios than we do, but when you add pensions and Medicare, they are far worse off than us.

For example, people highlight how Europe cares for citizens with free medical care for everyone. But they fail to see the bill that is now due. Most European countries are running out of funds much faster than we are, having already printed themselves into hyperinflation.

Not paying for these entitlement services for the elderly and sick would collapse a country. Hiking taxes only goes so far. At what point is a sovereign nation eating up all of the output of its population, allowing no monetary freedom?

The only choice is to print. That is the only mathematical solution. So every developed nation does it. This protects the system's elite (or rather the unproductive class) and allows governments to keep rulers in power.

As long as it appears bad but not bad enough, citizens will cope. At least they have each other to commiserate. Eventually, wage earners and retirees are crushed from this debt beyond repair.

What good is free medical care if the other necessities of life double and triple every year?

No merchant or vendor wants to raise prices on customers. You want to make more money as an entrepreneur, small business owner, or CEO of a publicly-traded company. But this is accomplished as you become more efficient. You streamline, achieve economies of scale, negotiate better deals, and increase volume.

Within reason, you have to find the right price point to define who your customers or clients are. But once you have them, you don't increase prices unless you are increasing value. Otherwise, your business will ultimately fail.

You might scratch your head because you've been conditioned to accept rising prices. But this is not the norm. It is the fix to a broken system.

Prices increase out of necessity. Companies issue public apologies when they have to raise prices. Businesses shrug their shoulders and say, "sorry, it's inflation."

The cost of labor, supplies, transportation, and materials go up, so they transfer to the consumer to generate the same profit margin for the company.

Price inflation is a response to money supply inflation. Prices have no choice but to adjust up when there's more money in the system. In the short term, other forces like supply chain issues, weather, and logistics are at play. Politicians love to point these out as the cause.

But in the long term, inflation is simply more money chasing the same amount of goods and services.

The price tag of that slice of pizza is a nominal metric for the degradation of our time reserves. But no one tells us that our time has depleted 20%. They tell us that the slice of pizza will now cost 20% more. This is inflation branding.

Extending the pizza analogy, picture a pie with 10 slices representing an economy's entire output. All of its labor, goods, services, and property are represented by those 10 slices. You have title to 1 slice of this pizza. This gives you 10% of the entire economy.

Imagine that the government comes in and re-slices the 10-slice pizza into 20 slices. Now there are more slices for everyone. This is good, right? But notice that no new pizza was added. And since you held title to 1 slice, your prior 10% share is now cut in half to 5% (1 slice of 20 slices = 5%).

If you want to return to your prior 10% ownership of the pizza network, you must purchase an additional slice to have 2 slices of the newly inflated 20-slice economy. Thus, you are spending more to have the same amount of calories and food content as before.

When the Federal Reserve inflates the money supply, they aren't adding more "pizza." They aren't adding more economic output associated with the currency increase. The economy merely gets resliced to get repriced.

Inflation reduces our percentage of the monetary network without any action on our part. It directly slashes whatever share we have worked to obtain.

Similar to currency conversion when we travel to another country, inflation converts our currency to itself using higher numbers. $1 converts to $1.10 with 10% inflation. The value received for that $1.10 is the same as when it was $1.

We get inflation of units, not value. This wouldn't be bad if inflation levels for all goods, services, property, and labor rose in conjunction with each other.

But inflation isn't equal across sectors. It steals our time at different rates in different categories.

Wages and labor rates rarely rise in line with consumer goods or assets. The long-term effect is over-consumption and more debt on less inflationary, cheap, disposable products.

Many need that 18% credit card for lack of a savings system to equally grow at 18%. Their wages might rise 5% if they're fortunate. But their savings might be half that. Add in taxes, and actual rates reduce even more.

No one should need a raise. But we haven't known a world without inflation. Rather than a raise, everything we consume should become cheaper.
Technology and deflation naturally do this for us, as demonstrated in the
prior chapter.

When we earn, we have income tax. When we spend, we have sales tax.
When we invest, we have capital gains tax. When we start a business, we
have business and payroll tax. Even if we decide to give away our money,
we have a gift tax. Then when we die, we have an estate tax. And if we are
fortunate enough to save, we get inflation tax.

Inflation is the worst tax because it does not occur at the transaction. We
don't see it as a line item. There's no transparency. It's more of a default tip
we don't get to choose.

Governments and their central banks acknowledge inflation. They regularly publish inflation figures and openly talk about it. But they craft
and mince their words to continue the charade that rising inflation isn't
a problem.

In the U.S., consumers often think price inflation occurs slowly enough to
deal with it. But it is faster than we think. The BLS (Bureau of Labor and
Statistics) publishes the "official" inflation rate that the government and
Federal Reserve base all of their monetary policy - the CPI.

The CPI (Consumer Price Index) measures a "basket of goods" to give
investors and Wall Street an idea of what a typical consumer's inflation rate
looks like for purchases.

This in itself is a terrible measure. Who is a typical consumer? One person's
"basket" is not another's.

We hear that inflation is officially 9% or 10%. This is ridiculously high. Yet even these numbers are manipulated lower than the actual rate.

The official inflation rate skews with sleight of hand, often due to politics. When certain products or sectors of an economy inflate faster than others, those are removed and replaced with lower price increases.

The index for which we are supposed to compare inflation from one period to another comprises cherry-picked goods. It negates proper comparisons from one period to the next.

When the price of fish is up 30%, fish is removed from the food portion of the basket and replaced with cheaper, farmer-subsidized products. It keeps the CPI artificially low. Also, when fish is too expensive, consumers buy less of it, thus removing its impact from the calculation.

Medical costs in the CPI get reduced to maintenance care and ignore the actual costs of insurance companies. Housing prices are entirely removed and replaced by rental rates. Oil and gas are subsidized by federal and state or pumped from sovereign reserves in an "energy-printing" strategy.

This has exceptions and nuances, but this is approximately how official inflation numbers are collected and re-calculated to reduce the actual rate.

Politicians want inflation to be as low as possible. It never looks good. In September of 2022 President Biden went on national TV (*60 Minutes*) to say that inflation was looking good. It hadn't gone up in the last month. Inflation was still "only 8.5%. Same as last month."

True, it had not gone up *in that month*. But it was still at a reported 8.5%. In other words, U.S. citizens' wealth was still evaporating at a rate of 8.5% a year. I don't fault Biden. He's fed the same manipulation we are.

The government's own reported inflation figures during this period (November 2021 to November 2022) showed food in elementary and secondary schools up 250%, fuel and oil up 65%, airline fares up 36%, flour up 25%, and public transportation up 23%. But because of basket manipulation, we arrive at a weighted average of 8.5%.

Whether official or not, true inflation rates are always personal regardless of the CPI. If you are in the market for a house and sending your kids to school, your inflation rate might be 30 or 40%, depending on geography and academics.

But did the university, the professors, or the curriculum become 30 to 40% more valuable this year than one year ago?

Did that new 4-bedroom house magically grow 2 more bedrooms overnight? Or is that new house the same new house as before? Actually, now that house is one year older. It has depreciated. Why is it more expensive? Shouldn't it be less? Materials decay.

If you live in someone's back garage, play video games, and eat frozen pizzas, your inflation rate might be closer to the official CPI. The cost of your basket of goods might be 7% or whatever the reported rate is.

Sadly, the basket of goods tends to capture lower income and less healthy spending habits, like processed foods with industrial seed oils. This helps keep the official rate low.

But most might have a personal inflation rate of 25% or more. That $10 cocktail is now $12.50. It seems small and acceptable, yet that's 25%. My coffee brand is up 35% in the last 12 months. But do I care when a $2 cup becomes $2.70? Not really.

How much has your education costs risen? What about flights, home utilities, dinners, cars, pets, movies, concerts, hotels, auto repairs, furniture, medical insurance, computers, clothes, or a hamburger? Most financial analysts will tell you the actual CPI is at least double the officially reported rate. That would put inflation at over 18% at the time of publication.

Post C-19, reported CPI reached 9.1% due to rampant money printing. At that rate, losing half of your purchasing power takes just under 5 years. If the double rule for true inflation applies, 18% cuts your savings by 50% in under 2.5 years.

Said another way, what you can purchase today for $10,000 will cost you $15,000 in 2.5 years. And in 20 years, you will have lost 99% of your purchasing power.

The CPI was reported to be in the 2 to 3% range for decades. It was said to be a normal, healthy target. But even at these synthetically low rates, inflation cuts your purchasing power in half 14 years later.

Inflation's effect on your money is reverse compounding. It's an exponential rot instead of growth. Your portfolio numbers go up, so you are winning on paper. But those numbers are in a tug-of-war with inflation's negative compounding effect.

Traditional finance advisors tell their clients that Bitcoin is an inflation hedge, at least the ones who are smart enough to learn it's not a scam. They say Bitcoin is insurance against the value deterioration of fiat.

But Bitcoin isn't a hedge. Bitcoin is a solution.

Once technology allowed electronic signatures, DocuSign or other digital signing software didn't become insurance for the fax machine. It replaced it altogether. People didn't mostly use their fax machine, but have DocuSign as an insurance backup just in case the machine fails.

Bitcoin is the improvement. It's the advancement away from an obviously archaic and broken system. It offers a way to escape inflation even if the government keeps inflating.

18

PROOF OF LIABILITY

"How, sir, would you make a ship sail against the wind and currents by lighting a bonfire under her deck? I have not the time to listen to such nonsense."

Napoleon Bonaparte, when told about the steamboat

*N*ominal rates are the published rates of investments. *Real rates* are what you actually receive regarding what you can purchase. The only rates that materially matter are real rates since they factor in inflation. But everyone fixates on nominal rates.

If salmon swam at 3 miles per hour upstream, that would be the nominal rate. It's how fast salmon can swim. But the real rate factors in the speed of the opposing stream at 2 miles per hour. Thus the real rate of a salmon's migration upstream is only 1 mile per hour.

If money is important, then nominal rates are essential. But if what money can buy is important, then nominal rates are meaningless.

Everyone fixates on the wrong metric.

The world's largest investment asset and most widely owned investment product is our U.S. treasury bonds, most notably the 10-year U.S. treasury bond (USTB).

USTBs sell to buyers as "risk off" assets. When all other investment vehicles are crashing or wildly fluctuating, the safest place to go to de-risk is into bonds.

For the uninitiated, bonds are how the government borrows money. Period. They issue 2, 5, 10, 15, 20, or 30-year bonds (10-year being the most popular).

The government gets a lump sum of cash from investors when they sell a USTB. Investors get a fixed percentage rate as income and their returned principal at the end of the period.

States and cities, corporations, and start-ups, all issue bonds. Just about any entity that needs a loan issues bonds. It is why bonds are considered low risk as they aren't investments per se. They are loans.

Bonds don't fluctuate with the performance of the entity or sovereign. They are strictly fixed loans with fixed terms. And they get paid back before those entities' investors.

But bonds are net losses against an inflationary environment. And this is how most of the world "saves" in a tool guaranteed to lose from the outset. There isn't a chance one can make money with bonds, not when the government is printing money.

The old 60/40 stock/bond portfolio mix that licensed RIAs (Registered Investment Advisors) recommend is no longer valid. It used to be investing 101: put 60% of your money into stocks and 40% into bonds.

Historically, stocks return triple or even quadruple what bonds do. But they are much more volatile. They can go years with negative returns. So a safe mix has always advised a large chunk of bonds to secure your main principal, but with as much stock allocation as you can stomach to grow it.

Typically the younger you are, the advice says to skew this 60/40 percentage more in favor of stocks, like 70/30 or even 80/20. And the older you are, the more you lean into bonds, like 50/50 or 40/60, taking more risk off the table, so your money is there in retirement.

But bonds have yet to hurdle the rate of true inflation in decades. They negate whatever increase you can make on the stock side.

At least with an 80/20 mix, only 20% of your portfolio is guaranteed to lose with bonds. The other 80%, although volatile due to the nature of stocks, has a winning chance against inflation.

The government needs to borrow your personal capital because they have a deficiency. They have generated less tax revenue than they are spending in Medicare, Medicaid, and the military, so they need your surplus.

Since a bond is a loan to the government from you, they want the interest rates they have to pay on that debt as low as possible. You equally want your mortgage rate as low as possible when you're borrowing for a house - no different. A borrower obviously wants low rates.

But when the borrower is the government, they can set these rates at whatever they want. They do this by adding more money into the supply.

When there's more money in the supply, banks are forced to lower interest rates to attract consumers. It entices more borrowers to leverage money through business loans, mortgages, and government bonds.

Conversely, lower bond rates negatively affect all retirees and "savers" who are heavily weighted into bonds. Inflation may help the government's debt problem but worsens pensioners' retirement goals. Those saving in a supposedly off-risk asset to avoid volatility have a guaranteed leak.

If a bond investment pays 2%, but inflation is 10%, you are guaranteed to lose 8% of the value of that investment each year you hold it. That negative 8% is the real rate, not the published nominal rate of 2%.

It's one thing to chase the best interest rates possible, but without factoring inflation into the equation, it's idiotic and pointless, just like saying salmon can swim 3 miles per hour upstream.

Let's assume you invest (lend the government) $10,000 in a USTB and get a 2% interest rate for the next 10 years. It is a very typical investment product sold to most of the world.

This $10,000 investment represents earned resources that you, the investor, don't need today but would like returned in 10 years. You benefit the economy by allowing someone else to leverage your resources.

With this 10-year bond, you receive 2% of your locked-up $10,000 each year for the 10-year duration. The rate doesn't go up or down. It is fixed. At the end of the 10th year, you get your $10,000 principal back.

Unlike typical amortized loans (like your home mortgage), bonds delay the entire principal amount until the end of the period.

With this trade, you arrest the opportunity of your $10,000 in resources for a whole decade. Anything else you could have built or experienced with that money is put on hold. You take that risk.

As compensation, you nominally receive your 2% interest, which is $16.67 monthly. But with inflation at 10%, you pay the government $66.66 per month to hold it for you. That's the hurdle rate of 8% (10% inflation less 2% interest).

It gets worse. This only accounts for the inflation on the interest portion of the bond, not the $10,000 principal.

Sticking with 10% inflation (again, your personal rate is probably double this), you will need $26,000 in 10 years' time to purchase the same goods that $10,000 could buy you before you bought the bond to begin with. You've fallen $13,000 short in spending power with this 10-year trade!

Here's the real story investment advisors do not tell you:

Pay the government $49.99 monthly for 10 years ($66.66 monthly inflation less $16.67 interest). At the end of 10 years, pay them $13,000. There is no difference between this story and the actual one regarding what you can buy today with $10,000 versus in 10 years. And that's all that matters.

Of course, your alternative is to sit in cash. But then your money is debased even more. In cash, you get hit with inflation but don't have the interest accumulation of bonds to dampen its impact.

In 1981 the official CPI was over 10%. But at the time, bonds paid over 14%. So as high as inflation was, you could earn a 4% real rate. It was certainly more attractive than our modern economy.

But we will never return to numbers like this. We have too much debt on our balance sheet. The government would default if bonds went any-where near 5 or 6%. They can't make those high-interest payments, just like homeowners couldn't make their mortgage payments in 2008 when mortgages shot up.

Our largest national expense is the interest we have to pay on our debt. Just the interest! At publishing, there is almost $32 trillion saved in USTBs. That is a massive amount of wealth stored in a losing proposition.

The entire world saves in our bonds, partly due to the start of the petrodol-lar system we set up in 1971. So this wealth depletion isn't solely on our shores. Unfortunately, it affects those outside our borders at an exponen-tially more devastating rate than us. They can't print money as we can, or their currency is tied to ours.

Whereas developed nations like the U.S. or Japan can print money to pay their debts, developing countries don't have that option. They are loaned billions of dollars in USD, so they must save and pay their debts in USD.

As we inflate our money supply, the cost of Argentina, Lebanon, or Turkey's debt in dollars exceeds ours by multitudes. They survive on our loans in USD, which only enslaves them with USD debt. We decrease their purchasing power by inflating the currency they have to pay us back.

We build our entire lives to save for an imagined future. However, inflation erases the integrity of that future, and at a rate faster than we can save for it.

This keeps us working, which keeps us paying taxes. For foreign countries, it keeps them "compliant" with us. They need our money to pay back our money.

It is why the IMF (International Monetary Fund), the World Bank, and the WEF (World Economic Forum) seem generous on the surface but are really governance mechanisms to pillage and suppress developing nations.

When inflation gets too high, governments attempt to reverse inflation. It only partially works because they can't afford the higher interest rates. But in the short term, the government raises rates to tighten the supply.

Savers and pensioners benefit from higher rates on their savings accounts and bonds. Their fixed incomes go up. It helps the lower class and poor who depend on cash. But higher rates mean companies can't hire, and unemployment typically goes up. Again, it hurts the lower class and the poor.

But when rates go back up, mortgages become expensive. Real estate suffers as less people can afford the payments. Stocks suffer because investors leave the risk of stocks for more conservative savings accounts.

This is the government's pickle, all due to fiat's ability to manipulate and print. Fiat has given the government privileges no one should have over the wealth of others. Although seemingly helpful at first, these advantages transfer liability from the Central Bank to the rest of the world.

Investments denominated with inflationary currency force us to seek ever more risk to stay in front of this time theft. But the higher the rate of return, the higher the liability. In the face of inflation, is the risk ever worth it?

Debt holders are paid first when entities go bankrupt, whether the government, a municipality, or a company. So people with bonds are in first position. They have the least amount of risk.

Stocks take on more risk. They lose out during a bankruptcy. Stockholders are paid back only if anything remains after bondholders and other secured creditors are made whole first.

To rise above stock rates, you have to move into real estate, partnerships, start-ups, or other direct ownership vehicles that are less passive. Depending on the structure of those investments, it requires active roles of running a business, management, maintenance, problem-solving, etc.

All savings and investment products are liabilities.

Bonds are a loan we make to an entity. But bonds fail. Cities have gone bankrupt and defaulted - ditto for companies. Savings accounts are rehypothecated by banks. If everyone showed up to get their money, the bank would shut down, as they have done many times.

Countries like Venezuela, Lebanon, China, Brazil, and Argentina have completely closed retail banks. In 2022 citizens in Lebanon robbed banks at gunpoint to demand the release of their own money.

PayPal, one of the largest online banks, sent out notices that they would charge U.S. customers $2,500 if anyone violated their policies. This included posting misleading information on social media. Yes, here in the U.S. where we have free speech, where people debate topics, and some make mistakes.

Other finance apps are known to confiscate the money of sex workers or medical marijuana facilities or ban them from using their services.

Banks confiscate or censor users based on politics or activism. The liability is trust of the bank, trust that their counterparty risk is secure. And if our principal remains intact, there's inflation. Inflation is a liability.

Stocks have liability. They can flat-out go to zero when a company goes under. They are susceptible to wild swings, product rollouts, legal troubles, rumors, etc. There's a single point of failure, if not at least a centralized one.

Everything that Wall Street trades is a liability. There is someone you can sue for every product or security. Someone is accountable for management decisions. And the riskier the product, the higher the liability.

But everything Wall Street seeks and trades gives them priority. They have insider information. They are tied to politics, big banks, and thus early information.

The liability is for those in the second chair (you and me), and the greater cost is for those in the third chair who are priced out of investment assets due to income or geography.

Real estate is the ultimate liability.

With real estate, you owe the bank, or they take it from you. You owe the county property taxes, or they take it from you.

Real estate is liable to deterioration and depreciation. It isn't portable or divisible. It's highly illiquid.

With real estate, there are too many third parties you need to trust to locate it, acquire it, secure it, administer it, and transfer it.

If you're an investor, there's the liability that tenants won't pay, and you have to evict. Evictions can take up to a year and sometimes longer.

There's also substantial risk with real estate due to industry fluctuations, population shifts, zoning changes, etc. Entire towns have been ruined and abandoned due to political decisions. In other words, real estate isn't borderless.

Just look at Detroit's over 60% population shrink from 1960 to 2010 due to politics and industrialization policies - same for St. Louis, Pittsburgh, and Cleveland.

And then there's privacy. People know if you own real estate.

Bitcoin has no physical depreciation. There is no need for someone to manage it for you. It is already diversified across every asset class as it represents money itself. It's cost-efficient with no minimum barrier to entry.

For those with the mindset and mettle, there's running your own business. It is the most rewarding of traditional finance routes but also the most challenging with the most liabilities. Employees, loans, lawsuits, insurance, marketing, taxes, customer complaints, compliance, and cash flow - feed into daily (and nightly) liability of your wallet and well-being.

I'm a fan of many of these investments and have touted them for years. My last book is mostly about them. But it's because I've been doing everything possible to lose *less* due to inflation. I wouldn't have this concern if it were not for fiat as our monetary token. But I will be put in jail if I don't pay taxes in fiat, which forces me to acquire more fiat.

Fiat has the greatest liability of all. We are liable on investments denominated in fiat as outlined above and then liable a second time to permission, manipulation, and inflation. It's the inflation rate itself that often originates the liability on these products.

Any time there is an interest rate on anything, there is a liability and risk.

Traditional investments are all liabilities. If it weren't for inflation, we wouldn't have to take such high risks in the first place.

We have enough liability in our lives. Relationships, family, and career dynamics alone are a daily liability. Our money shouldn't be or shouldn't have to be.

People who contribute to a society's economy should have the option to store their excess output in hard money, not one susceptible to liability on top of the liability they overcame to acquire the money.

Bitcoin is the first asset in history that has no liability. There is no other party to be liable to. No one is on the other side of Bitcoin other than code. And that code only solidifies that Bitcoin is unconditionally and unquestionably yours.

Whenever there is a system that requires trust, it is a liability.

Here in the U.S. there is a multi-trillion dollar economy with police, attorneys, judges, courts, jails, and our entire military-industrial complex. We have an elaborate infrastructure of punishment and force in lieu of trust.

These controls are necessary to protect the magical money printer of the Central Bank. This genie lamp is so prized that the world swings and sways to its activity. And everyone knows that the Fed has unlimited wishes.

19

PROOF OF INK

"Stock prices have reached a permanently high plateau."

Yale economist, Irving Fisher, 1929 (the Dow Jones was at 381, and has since climbed 100 times over)

If money printing generated real wealth for a nation, then places like Zimbabwe, Venezuela, Turkey, Lebanon, or Brazil would be the wealthiest nations in the world. But as history has proven, inflating your citizen's currency ultimately leads to its financial collapse.

This isn't just a modern day occurrence. There has always been a "money printer." And because of it, there has always been hyperinflation that has collapsed empires, whether the Roman Empire or the Ottoman Empire.

As far back as the 4th century B.C., emperors couldn't resist the temptation to substitute silver with cheaper metals such as nickel or copper.

The Roman Empire was famous for melting down their coins and reconstructing them with less and less silver. Their silver denarius coin went from having a 95% silver concentration to less than 5% over a 200-year period.

Those who were tight with, and close to, the bankers and politicians enjoyed the re-minting of coins. They didn't have to work for their money. They could bolster their lifestyle and enslave others to work for them.

The Pyramids of Egypt, the Roman Colosseum, the Great Wall of China, the Taj Mahal, and even Stonehenge were all largely built off the backs of people who couldn't afford decency or debt due to inflation.

If it were not for the money printer there would not be slaves, at least not nearly to the extent seen throughout history.

Like all of these failures of humanity, Roman coin melting shifted proof of work to proof of force. Eventually people lost trust in the empire which led to its demise. Rome's soldiers weren't willing to fight for worthless coins.

In England, King Henry VIII became known as, "Old Copper Nose." He wanted to pay for England's wars without taxing his citizens. So he had his minters "clip" coins by shaving down their circumference. The silver coins, or the pounds, were initially named for the weight of silver they contained. They kept their name but not their silver.

When it was apparent coins were getting smaller, King Henry switched to melting down the coins and replacing them with cheaper metals. It kept them from shrinking, but their value was debased. There was less silver in them, thus less value.

The pound no longer had a pound of silver in it, making its name completely obsolete. This began the shift from money (real silver) to fiat currency.

Similar to what we witnessed with Presidents Roosevelt and Nixon, King Henry depegged and repegged money in a tangible and comedically visible way.

Due to his ego, King Henry had his entire face front and center on every coin, rather than the typical profile. But the re-minted silver coating was so thin that it would rub off, exposing King Henry's big nose at the outermost point on the coin. Coins soon revealed a small copper dot on his nose; thus, the nickname "old copper nose" was born.

Citizens knew when they saw the King's red nose on their coins that they were being lied to and stolen from.

The Magna Carter, signed in 1215 by King John, stated that its people could not be taxed without a vote. Taxing citizens required approval and permission. This law still exists in parliament today.

But no different than our modern-day currency, money printing circumvents this law. When you can print money, there is no need for a vote on taxes. And thus, the pound is no longer correlated to an actual pound of silver, just as the dollar is no longer correlated to gold.

People hate when you tax them but love when you give them free money. Both have the same effect. One allows the government to spend money for citizens. The other allows citizens to spend it for the government. One is short-term, and one is long-term. In the end, they are identical.

The Greek dictator in Syracuse, Dionysius, the Elder, also skirted these tax laws most blatantly. He simply re-stamped all drachma coins with a "2" on their face without having to melt down or reconstitute coins. Citizens lined up at banks, brought in their coins, had them stamped, and then went home with the same number of coins.

But now every coin in circulation was suddenly worth 2 drachmas instead of the original 1 drachma. Dionysius inflated the entire currency by 100%, doubling it. But as you can see, quite literally, no one had any more money. It was just re-stamped by force of the dictator.

By doubling the sovereign reserves, Dionysius could pay for his wars. He had twice as much money. But the economy of Syracuse quickly adjusted and doubled its prices.

People knew that 5 drachma coins were 5 drachma coins regardless if they contained a "1" or a "2" on them. They still wanted those 5 coins, which were now 10 drachmas - the same number of coins, double the price.

It's baffling that anyone thought this was sustainable. But here we sit today, repeating history only with methods more sophisticated than stamping, clipping, or remelting.

Today, we effectively walk into the bank with 10 bucks and come out with 20 bucks. Yet those 20 bucks buy the same value of goods as the 10 bucks we had before we walked in.

Currency printing is a contemporary version of this debasement that started thousands of years ago. Instead of an emperor, a king, or a dictator, we now have central banks. And instead of stamping, we simply have more currency.

The U.S.'s Central Bank is The Federal Reserve, or simply "The Fed." It is a private company. It's owned and run by private citizens. They are not elected officials, yet they control the money supply of the U.S. and thus the world.

This is where obfuscation and confusion begin for most since "Fed" sounds like "federal government." But there's the government, and separately there's The Fed. One is based on democracy and votes. The other is just a company formed by citizens to make money - literally make money.

Where the government dirties its hands is in the arrangement they have with this private corporation. The government appoints the only people who can run The Fed. Again, not elected.

The President of the United States selects 7 individuals to be on the Board of Governors. Those 7 people oversee the 12 big Federal Reserve regional banks that geographically cover the U.S.

All retail banks, the ones you and I walk into to send a wire or cash a check, have relationships with one of these 12 Federal banks based on geography. It is the only way to gain a bank charter and offer FDIC insurance to customers.

Some say the office of the President's most important job is appointing judges to the Supreme Court. And many vote for the President solely on this basis. But few consider that the President picks The Fed chair and the Board of Governors.

As crucial as many issues of our country are, they are all downstream of money.

Money influences the environment, politics, trade, immigration, retirement, medical care, education, etc. Fiat is the root cause of the limitations, challenges, and problems these issues face.

The decisions available to a central bank are an absolute superpower with moral hazards. Accordingly, The Fed chairman, Jerome Powell, holds the most powerful position globally. It's more powerful than the President.

Those 10-year U.S. treasury bonds (USTBs) the entire world holds value in are stored at commercial banks, like Vanguard, Fidelity, or Wells Fargo, by the investors who purchase them there.

When our government wants to stimulate the economy, they inflate the money supply by buying as many bonds back from investors as possible.

This process takes the bond certificate away from the investor and gives them liquid cash in its place. Even though the investor has the same investment value, they are more apt to go out and spend with cash sitting in their checking account than a bond on their portfolio statement.

But since bonds are government debt, they want to maintain a certain amount of "monetary integrity" by not directly buying their own debt, even though that's exactly what they are doing by purchasing their own bonds.

Nevertheless, the government uses their special relationship with The Fed to conceal this magic.

The government tells The Fed to go to commercial banks and buy their investors' bonds. The Fed makes attractive offers such that current bondholders will sell. Bondholders can make more money by selling rather than waiting the full 10 years until maturity of the bond.

Now The Fed owns the bond, and thus the government makes interest payments to The Fed, instead of to the prior investor.

This process doubles the money of the bond. Printing!

At a $10,000 value, for example, the bond is now an asset on the Fed's balance sheet. They'll collect interest from the government on it for the next 10 years.

But at the same time, the investor now has $10,000 in cash since they sold the bond to The Fed. So the prior $10,000 bond the investor held at the bank has now just turned into a total of $20,000 in value.

The Fed never had to generate any of this money, yet they now hold the bond, an asset to collect money from the government.

Here's how this is accomplished:

The government types out additional zeros on a computer screen to add to The Fed's balance sheet, who then distributes those same zeros to commercial banks' balance sheets.

The Commercial banks then, in turn, buy the bonds from investors and send the bonds back to The Fed. Operation Money Print complete.

The Fed receives magical "money" that didn't exist before and wasn't generated from any economic activity. It isn't tied to any real-world productivity. The government just wished it into existence.

This is the core of how fiat is distorted and manipulated through money printing. It is sometimes called Quantitative Easing. The Fed has just eased (meaning inflated) the quantity of our money supply.

The government wants investors to spend that liquid cash. The logic is that a river with more water should ideally spill over and form new little rivers.

Similar to when you sell a house and convert that paper equity into actual cash, you are more likely to go out and celebrate and purchase more goods and services, even if you don't necessarily need them.

You feel flush and wealthy after a big sale, even though you have the same value of wealth. Before, your wealth was on paper, on a Zillow or Redfin screen. After the sale, it's liquid cash burning a hole in your pocket.

Here's the rub: Most don't spend all of that cash. Most only spend a fraction of that and stash the rest back into their bank accounts. This is where fractional banking injects the magical money printer with steroids.

Banks have to keep a minimal amount of customers' deposits on hand. Historically this has been roughly 10%. This low percentage is a disaster, as we've seen from bank runs throughout the world.

The Great Depression of the 30s saw citizens lose their deposits as banks closed and froze withdrawals. Banks had a tiny fraction of what they said they had.

This theft happened again in Argentina in 2001, Iceland in 2008, Zimbabwe in 2009, Cyprus in 2013, Greece in 2015, Venezuela in 2016, China in 2021, and Lebanon in 2022.

It is bound to happen again when banks hold only 10% of the money they are supposed to have. But when the government wants to inflate the money supply, they encourage The Fed to lower this requirement even more.

When C-19 hit, The Fed immediately lowered this reserve requirement to 0%. Not a single penny of any depositor's money had to be held by the bank. Banks were encouraged to lend out the entirety of a depositor's money to someone else.

But as an FDIC member bank, the bank need not worry. The Fed can easily add more zeros to any member bank.

The FDIC insures over $9 trillion of deposits in banks. But they hold only $125 billion in assets. That means 98.6% of all bank money is at risk if everyone were to go in the same day and empty their accounts.

When you hear the media talk about The Fed raising or lowering rates, it's really the Fed Funds Rate they refer to. All other interest rates are downstream and adjusted in line with this rate.

The Fed Funds Rate is the rate at which commercial banks borrow from each other to meet the reserve requirements. If the Fed requires banks to keep 5% in reserves and there are $1,000,000 in deposits at a bank, they need to have $50,000 on hand each night the bank closes.

Banks are good at getting as close to that figure as possible, as they effectively lose money when cash is sitting in their vaults. In this case, they would lend out $950,000 and keep only $50,000 in their safe.

If one night a bank's vault has only $30,000, they must immediately borrow $20,000 from another member bank in overnight lending. So when the Fed lowers this rate, banks borrow more and thus loan more - more arbitrage for banks to earn money.

Adjusting this rate is what encourages fractional reserve banking. When this rate is lowered banks load up on more cash to issue more business loans, construction loans, and mortgages.

This rate adjustment injects more money into the economy and exponentially compounds the money supply since most of this value sits at a bank. The bank then lends it out again, again, and again.

Let's return to the original $10,000 cash an investor received for selling their bond back to The Fed. We know at that point the money was doubled - $10,000 cash to the investor, and a $10,000 asset to the Fed that the government now owes.

Next, an investor stashes $9,000, for example, at the bank and spends the other $1,000 on stuff, just as the government intended. Due to fractional banking and the lowering of The Fed Funds rate, the bank that holds the investor's $9,000 will now lend that portion out.

That new borrower of the $9,000 maybe only needs $1,000 and deposits the remaining $8,000 into their bank. Now the new borrower's bank loans out that $8,000. And so on and so on. $7,000. $6,000. $5,000. Etc.

This re-loaning process became an infinite money machine that started with only a $10,000 loan, initially printed by the Fed. But this one $10,000 loan, in this example, becomes $9,000 + $8,000 + $7,000... down to the last $1,000. This repetition creates $45,000 in additional money by all of those deposits from borrowers.

Thus, the original $10,000 bond held by an investor became $20,000 + $45,000. So $65,000 was created from the original buy-back of the bond.

None of this money existed before. And it didn't enter the supply due to economic output. It's all just credit.

But this $65,000 isn't done multiplying. There's more.

When a borrower deposits money in a bank, it's an asset to the depositor. It can be used as collateral to buy additional assets. The customer can collateralize any cash deposit, without actually spending it, to, in turn, borrow to buy a business, a home, or a car, for example.

All the Fed did was purchase bonds from banks and adjusted The Fed Funds Rate to allow banks to hold less cash and lend more out. That cash found its way into the economy with new businesses, new mortgages, more hiring, and then back to the government in the form of taxes for all those activities.

That's what *really* happens. It's just easier to call it money printing.

Now the government can pay for their programs, fund entitlements, and stay within budget since this activity generates taxes. Although that's a lie, they can't stay on budget, which is why they keep printing.

The government is wildly over-budget and in a huge deficit every year. So they issue more bonds to make their debt payments. They issue more debt to pay more debt. These bonds are the government's surrogate printer ink that inflates away a nation's debt at taxpayers' expense.

Money printing is magical when the Federal Reserve has unlimited funds to buy as many bonds as the government asks. But since bonds are government debt, what happens when the bill comes due?

Once again, here's where this unique relationship distorts human time and action. The Fed will never foreclose on the government. The government appointed The Fed Chair and Board of Governors in the first place with cushy, well-paying jobs.

Thus The Fed isn't going to hire a collection agency or put a lien on The U.S. Treasury. Rather, The Fed simply buys more bonds, but this time directly from the government itself.

Since the government is the one who issues bonds, all they have to do is give The Fed the cash to buy the bonds. Now the government is flush with cash. They can bypass the investors and citizens altogether. No need for a vote.

This scheme is equivalent to getting a second credit card to pay the first credit card. And then getting a third credit card to pay the second, and so on.

Japan is a perfect example of this debt spiral as they directly buy their own JGBs (Japanese Government Bonds). This indulgence is why Japan has a 266% debt-to-GDP ratio. For every $1 of economic contribution, Japan incurs $2.66 in debt since they are buying their own debt to sustain their economy.

Greece is at 210% debt-to-GDP. Italy at 206%. Venezuela is at a whopping 350%.

In the U.S., we are at 140%. So for every $1 we generate in goods and services, we owe $1.40.

But the actual numbers are even worse because we don't really generate a full $1 in GDP. Over 65% of our GDP is our consumption rather than creation. We've turned into a country of bingers rather than builders.

This debt cycle never stops. Not in a fiat system with no immediate or apparent repercussions. This happens just slowly enough in the U.S. to be acceptable for decades at a time. But of late, we've opened up the valve. What used to be a trickle is now a flood.

We only have to look at what happened to Germany from 1919 to 1933. To pay for the costs of WWI, The Weimar Republic government of Germany printed its currency into the stratosphere, causing hyperinflation.

Famously, people had to carry wheelbarrows of money to buy a loaf of bread. Their cash became worthless by the day. Banks became insolvent. Savings erased. Pensions evaporated. And homelessness and poverty spread. Eventually, people used currency to keep a fire lit.

Hyperinflation, unfortunately, led to the rise of the Nazi party and Hitler's dictatorship. In other words, money printing caused a perverse control over human lives. All of this resulted from broken money - money that could be printed and thus inflated on its citizens.

You can only suppress and destroy the life force of humanity for so long before its people rebel, overthrow, or migrate and start a better system. But Germany didn't have Bitcoin. They had no obvious or easy choice.

Credit can (and should) be good. But healthy credit only works in a closed value system where its quantity is known and fixed.

When credit is created due to proof of work, it doesn't create inflation. But if it is based on money printing, no work is tied to it - that credit will debase all other money in the system.

If I have $10,000 that I've worked for and want to loan you, then I base my criteria on your ability to pay, and what that $10,000 means to me based on the work I had to perform to earn it. I adjust the level of interest I charge based on that criteria.

But if a bank is encouraged to lend free money from bond purchases and then lend it again due to fractional reserve banking, it perverts the value of that money elsewhere in the system that wasn't free. It debases and devalues the same money of someone else who worked for it.

The bank's $10k loan to a borrower does not equal my $10k to a borrower. But together, the $20k weakens the value of my $10k. It's like pouring dirty water into clean water. It makes all of the water bad.

If a car dealership receives $2 million in money printing (stimulus, cheap loans, tax incentives, subsidies), they pass this on to car buyers. They offer 0% car financing for the next 60 months.

Now buyers will pay more for a car than they otherwise could with the money they worked for. At 0%, who wouldn't take that deal? So if the dealer marks up the sticker $2k more than it otherwise would have been in a free market, a buyer accepts that increase knowing the 0% financing more than makes up for that premium. This incentive drives up the prices of all cars.

Free or cheap credit results in higher prices for everyone, whether they have to work for their money or it is given to them via money printing. But since we all have to hold and transact in the same fiat currency, those who don't get the free money (car buyers) are devalued, while those who receive the free money (car dealerships) are valued.

Money supply inflation creates price inflation.

Mortgages are one of the best examples of money printing and a tool The Fed often wields. Cheap mortgages allow investors to buy a massive asset at multitudes higher than they would ever spend on anything else in their life. The purchase price of a home no longer matters, only the monthly payments.

In a free market without The Fed manipulating rates, mortgage companies will adjust their rates based on borrower creditworthiness. But when The Fed forces banking rates so low and the money is cheap, mortgage lenders are incentivized to make more loans.

On top of that, the government insures 98% of all mortgages through their Fannie Mae and Freddie Mac loan programs. Mortgage lenders don't have to take the risk, even though they vet the borrowers.

Following a few simple guidelines, mortgage lenders sell off the mortgages in less than 30 days due to this government insurance.

The government and Fed will buy almost all mortgages (effectively a form of a bond) from lenders when they want to increase the money supply. So banks are happy to write riskier loans to offload for a quick commission immediately.

But we've witnessed the housing collapse of 2008. We've seen how real estate cycles ebb and flow. As professional investors, we can game this. But for the average working person, this is not a way to increase purchasing power - by treating homes as piggy banks.

Real Estate is usually worth more over the long term in USD terms. But that's because more units are in supply, so more units are required to correlate to the same house. No different than the re-stamping of the drachma from 1 to 2.

The Fed's printing is no less devious than the Irishman who brought more rai stones to the island of Yap or the European explorers who brought counterfeit Aggry beads to West Africa. In both cases, it enslaves its people due to inflation.

Central banks have financed the wars of Western and developed economies. Most of those wars would never have existed (or to the extent they did) if governments had to pay for them with currency tied to money, meaning proof of work.

Nevertheless, here in the U.S., we have an unelected, private corporation that has full authority to control the money supply and thus largely determines if we can afford war and how long we can fight. This absolves the government of that tremendous responsibility. It's not them. It's the Fed. It's our Central Bank.

Fortunately, there's a way to peacefully protest by unsubscribing from fiat's proof of ink system and into Bitcoin's proof of work. Bitcoin takes fiat's money printing waterfall and tightens the valve shut.

Bitcoin was invented to suppress this inhumane ability to steal people's time and invalidate their energy.

For you, it may not seem dire. But for most of the world, Bitcoin is literally saving lives. It is more than just an asset. It is a whole new monetary system that allows money to be free of this manipulation of human action.

20

PROOF OF DESTRUCTION

"By 2005 or so, it will become clear that the internet's impact on the economy has been no greater than the fax machine's."

Nobel Prize-winning economist Paul Krugman, 1998

P aul Krugman has been a critic of Bitcoin for a long time. He has called it "pointless and worthless." And billionaire Bill Gates said he doesn't buy Bitcoin "because it doesn't add to society."

These fine gentlemen live in a privileged, Western society where they benefit from the Cantillon effect of the money printer.

They need to see the second and third-order effects of fiat's inflation in developing nations. Fiat causes wealth and political divide here in the U.S. but absolute destruction outside our borders.

The first principal problem with many of the world's ills is broken money. It's broken money that initiates many of the issues Bill Gates attempts to solve with climate change, disease, and agriculture. Broken money leads to poor choices, crime, over-consumption, etc.

We rarely think about the oxygen we breathe. But if you're SCUBA diving and your air tank runs low on air, you think about oxygen. The Western elite are part of 2 billion people who stay forever safe and dry on land. But 6 billion of the world's 8 billion population are underwater and running out of air.

There have been over 750 currencies around the world since the 1700s. Over 80% of those have imploded. The other 20% are barely surviving with perpetual money printing. Currency evaporation is why CBDCs are sprouting up everywhere. Those will be the reset to wipe out the global debt crisis from over-printing.

Every monetary system ever established ultimately collapsed due to inflation. The Sumerians, Persians, Greeks, Romans, Italian states, and every monarch of England failed due to their proclivity to print, pay for wars, and enslave their people.

The nation-state defaults on its citizens' wealth by having everything they own redenominated into their new currency, just like the drachma stamping of "2"s on every coin. For many countries, this will mean turning in, say, 1,000 units of a physical currency to receive 1 digital one. Then with total surveillance and control, a government can "re-stamp" as much as they want.

A hundred years ago, Germany had to print money to pay for WWI reparations. They inflated their papiermark currency by 325,000,000%.

That's not a typo. It required 4.2 trillion papiermarks to make one U.S. dollar. Thus Germany defaulted and reset to the new rentenmark currency, wiping out most of the country's wealth.

After WWII, Hungary's highest-denominated currency was the 1,000 pengo. Two years later, they inflated their pengo so much that they needed to redenominate it at 100,000,000,000,000,000,000,000. That's 100 quintillion!

That number is difficult to imagine as we rarely hear of any number greater than a trillion. But jump to quadrillion and then quintillion, and you arrive at 18 zeros!

Hyperinflation at these levels doesn't discriminate between Bill Gates and a day laborer. Both will be wiped out. Inflation annihilates the cardiologists, finance brokers, and captains of industry across the board. There's no way to escape monetary enslavement if you were unlucky enough to be born into these economies.

In the late 1920s, Peru hyperinflated their currency, resetting it several times until it was worth 1 billionth of what it was 6 years prior. If you held 1 billion dollars in the bank, it now had the purchasing power of 1 dollar.

Thus if Bill Gates were worth $100 billion in Peru's currency in the 1920s, 6 years later he would be worth a single hundred dollar bill.

In the early 1990s, Yugoslavia's largest denomination was the 50,000 dinar note. But it inflated to a 2,000,000 note at 40 to 1. It eventually inflated again to the 10,000,000,000 note. Prices increased 1 quadrillion percent in just two years - over 100% daily inflation. Prices doubled from when you went to sleep to when you woke up.

Just 20 years ago, the peso in Argentina was 1 to 1 with our U.S. dollar. Today it requires over 600 pesos to convert to 1 dollar. The Argentinians' highest-denominated money of 1,000 pesos became a 5,000 peso note, then 10,000, then 100,000,000,000.

In Zimbabwe, the hyperinflation was so bad in the early 2000s that they effectively had no money and no means to trade whatsoever. Their dollars inflated by 11,000% in one year. So they replaced their old Zimbabwe dollars with new ones at 1 to 1,000 to reset them.

The African state hyperinflated the new Zimbabwe dollars such that they had to release a 240 million dollar bill. That soon became the 500 million dollar bill. And then 5 billion, 25 billion, 50 billion, and then a 100 billion dollar bill! Annual inflation was 500 quintillion percent. That's 13 billion percent inflation per month! And here in the U.S. we go nuts when annual inflation hits 8%.

Africa has some of the fastest-adopting Bitcoin countries, primarily due to oppression and politics. 15 of Africa's 55 countries are still monetarily colonized by France under the CFA franc. They are forced to contribute half their money to reserves held in France.

Even though the continent is rich in resources like gold, the colonized countries must send half of that gold to France (the figure is over 80% for Togo).

Colonialism keeps most of Africa's countries poor as they must legally use France's support, loans, exports, etc. This relationship benefits France's investors at the expense of Africa's cheap labor and resources. The curse of the Aggry slave beads somehow never went away.

Africans seek refuge in U.S. dollars but have to acquire them on the black market since they're not legally allowed to own them. They pay a 100% premium at 2 to 1. On top of the 80%+ inflation in many parts of Africa, this brings their actual inflation to over 160%.

Also, Africans can't send money from country to country within their continent. That would be like the U.S. barring us from sending money from state to state. This limits opportunity and limits consumers to price gouging.

Those fortunate enough to receive funds outside of Africa have had to use Western Union or MoneyGram, which eats up 10% of the $50 billion remitted annually.

In Nigeria, almost 70% of the population regularly has their assets frozen or seized. If you voice your political beliefs, you're one step away from total destruction of any wealth you may have.

Property, businesses, and even your house, can be swiped from you without a judge or jury. Citizens face death squads because they voice their opinion about their wealth depletion.

Nigeria is Africa's most populous country with over 200 million citizens. It's an economic force. There's infrastructure, schools, and big businesses. But over 80% of the country's revenue goes to paying debt.

In part, Nigeria's imposition of its own CBDC is to blame. The central bank of Nigeria is invalidating all paper cash. So faced with a CBDC that has complete control of the government or Bitcoin which has none, guess which one the people choose?

Over 30% of Nigerians now own and transact in Bitcoin daily. That's the highest percentage in the world for a country. This adoption is in the face of Bitcoin being legally banned. But people will find a way.

Even without an internet connection, remote tribes and villages can transact in Bitcoin using "feature phones" that connect with each other like SMS texting. Bitcoin's pure peer-to-peer system bypasses any centralized entity, so the government has no "company" to shut down.

The human spirit wants to flourish. Governments can't shut down hope.

Recently, remittances in Nigeria reached almost $18 billion, the majority of that riding on Bitcoin's rails to and from Nigerians, some of whom are relatives living outside its borders. For them, it isn't just an opt-out from debasement. It's a means of freedom from confiscation and censorship.

For example, you can download the Strike app and directly send as little as 5 cents or any amount in Bitcoin to anyone in Africa. No intermediary. No fees. The Bitcoin network instantly converts any currency to Bitcoin, transfers the value across borders to where it needs to go, and then converts it to any currency again.

Nigerians can now form political activist groups and access financial products from which their own naira and CBDCs are cut off. Bitcoin unlocks economic potential for dynamic and entrepreneurial Nigerians.

Former CEO and founder of Twitter, Jack Dorsey, has joined forces with Jay-Z to bring education to Africa to help develop Bitcoin adoption. Jack cited Africa and Bitcoin as his two main reasons for stepping down as CEO of Twitter.

He said, "Bitcoin changes absolutely everything. I don't think there's any-thing more important in my lifetime to work on."

Since this announcement, the Central African Republic has become the second country to make Bitcoin legal tender (behind El Salvador as the first). Other countries in Africa, like Ghana or Kenya, may be next.

Africa has 6 of the top 20 countries with the most peer-to-peer Bitcoin transaction volume - Kenya, Nigeria, Togo, South Africa, Ghana, and Tanzania.

Vietnam currently has the highest peer-to-peer volume of any country, which is no surprise when 69% of its citizens have no bank access.

In Venezuela, they've wiped out 14 zeros of their currency in the last 20 years. What one of their bolivars could buy you 20 years ago now takes 1 trillion bolivars. The pricing changes from hour to hour. The country doesn't even have enough literal cash for citizens to transact if they could. Their inflation rate from 2016 to 2019 was 54,000,000%.

Bill Gates and Paul Krugman can withstand true inflation levels of 14 to 20% in the U.S. They sit in entitled positions with valuable information. And since they're not citizens of Turkey, Cuba, Lebanon, or Nigeria, they aren't banned from owning U.S. dollars or property. They aren't forced to hold their wealth in a token that loses its entire value overnight due to fiat debasement.

Of our 330 million citizens in the U.S., only 12 million citizens have to take out payday loans to make ends meet. Those borrowers initiate loans for $375 and pay $520 in interest on top of that.

7 million of these Americans need banking rails. They need somewhere to cash their checks or get credit. So they take out loans as prepaid debit cards to pay rent and utilities. This haircut amounts to $90 billion yearly in transaction fees because they have no bank.

Money printing in the U.S. since 1900 has destroyed 98% of the dollar's value. Today's dollar value is 2% of what it was once worth.

The privileged (many of you reading this book) come to Bitcoin because of its "number go up" technology. But in other countries, they use Bitcoin to survive utter destruction. We may think in terms of wealth. Others think in terms of survival.

Bitcoin's principles show citizens in developing nations how to gain freedom from the tyranny, restrictions, and censorship of their economies, allowing them to retain what they earn so they can buy food and shelter.

Just 20 years ago in Argentina, they froze everyone's assets. Commerce collapsed, unemployment skyrocketed, and riots ensued. Most of the middle class was thrown into poverty overnight.

Argentina isn't a third-world country. Argentina is a modern-day, financialized, G-20 country with a population of over 45 million people. But social unrest due to inflation makes Argentina behave like a third-world country.

Imagine not being able to sell your stocks, real estate, or get cash out of your bank. Add to this the 80%+ inflation levels Argentina has had recently, and even the privileged of Argentina have become newly poor.

Is it any wonder that Argentina is now one of the top 10 world's highest per-capita adopters of Bitcoin?

I don't know if Bill Gates has heard that Bitcoin has literally saved lives in Afghanistan. The women there are beaten, tortured, and deprived of basic human rights. They aren't allowed to seek jobs or have a bank account. And the men (often relatives of the women) are the ones who confiscate their belongings and punish them.

If you want to go to college, you must take the university entrance exam, called "Kankor." There's no other way to attend. But the Taliban has banned all high school girls from taking the exam.

Fortunately, fearless Bitcoin advocates have taught Afghan women how to work online privately as data processors and transcribers. They get paid in Bitcoin to bypass the religious and social barriers that keep them second-class citizens.

Stories have emerged where Afghan Women who have saved in Bitcoin (and held during the dips without selling) now have wealth 100 times that of the average annual Afghan salary.

They have crossed borders into Europe to escape oppression and death threats, having all their valuables confiscated or stolen along the way. But corrupt guards and thieves can't steal what they don't know to look for.

The Taliban and terrorists will scavenge and take what gold and jewelry they can, leaving the women with tattered clothes and a few photographs. But 12 obscure words written on a piece of paper, sewn in clothes, or memorized, are all that is necessary to start life anew.

Sadly, Afghanistan is but one example. There are over 75 economies in the world that discriminate against women.

When your life is in jeopardy, 12 words can be a gift. If you can successfully memorize the alphabet, a song, or every member of your 3 favorite bands, you can remember 12 words representing your life's work.

Bitcoin is the one accessible and nonviolent way to regain sovereignty and privately flee borders with stored wealth.

Venezuela is one of the most oil and gold-rich countries, yet completely bankrupt. Their fiat currency is so weak and hyperinflating that the country can't organize to mine their own resources.

Gold is just sitting there to benefit Venezuela and its citizens. But no one can invest into a hyperinflating economy. Once again, the measuring tape keeps changing for a group trying to build a house. When yards become feet, and feet become inches, it's too chaotic to coordinate.

It's like trying to schedule a meeting when an hour holds 65 minutes one day and 80 minutes the next. How do you collaborate and conduct business when you can't agree on value or lose that value overnight?

Those holding Venezuelan bolivars have such strict withdrawal limits that families must use dozens of debit cards to buy daily essentials. And if you run into the local police, they regularly confiscate your money.

The country has few options itself to escape complete collapse. But Bitcoin can give its citizens worldwide access to any financial product and run freely without theft or seizure.

In Lebanon, the government limited the LBP (Lebanese pound) conversions to dollars to only $500 USD per person. That's not much due to their rapid inflation. On February 1, 2023, their central bank officially devalued their currency by 90% compared to the U.S. dollar.

In 2022 Lebanese citizens demanded their money at gunpoint from their own banks. These aren't criminals. These are desperate savers of a country that has hyperinflated their fiat. ATMs stopped dispensing cash, banks closed and replaced glass windows with metal, and tanks rolled in.

For the 4 million Lebanese stuck in their nation's fiat, their life savings are completely frozen. This is a blatant deprivation of freedom in an otherwise "free" country.

In 1980 it required 2.8 LBP to convert to $1. Today it requires 57,000 LBP to get a single $1. Over 75% of Lebanese families have to buy food on credit, further enslaving their future.

The wealthy in Lebanon have jumped into gold and real estate. But increasingly, they risk confiscation and seizure. Their only safe haven completely free and separate from any form of state interference is Bitcoin.

Lebanese are now adopting and transacting on Bitcoin's rails, where they can retain and access their wealth. They can move it at any time outside of Lebanon's capital controls.

By now, everyone knows about the peaceful protests in Canada during C-19. Canada is a modern, Western democracy. Yet those who exercised their legal rights to protest vaccine mandates for truckers had their accounts closed.

Even those who donated to help those with frozen accounts had *their* accounts frozen. They couldn't pay their mortgages or buy food. Most of these truckers were already vaccinated. But they wanted to exercise their rights to protest that it be mandated.

Prime Minister Justin Trudeau unilaterally issued these bank freezes without any permission from Canada's legislature. He decreed it. No vote whatsoever.

Meanwhile, Trudeau has printed so much since C-19 that he added more to Canada's national debt than all Prime Ministers before him combined.

Then the Russia-Ukraine war broke out. How did Russian citizens support their relatives and friends in Ukraine without being labeled terrorists? How did Ukrainians receive support cut-off from traditional finance rails?

Bitcoin was (and still is) used to allow Russians who don't side with Putin to escape the country without wealth confiscation. Those without Bitcoin who attempted to leave were deprived of their property rights.

And for those within the country, Bitcoin becomes an efficient and private transfer system. It offers a complete separation of money and state. Why should geopolitics decide what one can do with their hard-earned money?

For Canada, Russia, and Ukraine, Bitcoin is a savior. Bitcoin has already transferred hundreds of billions of dollars in monetary aid and relief to those cut off from banks and under surveillance by the government.

Everyone in Ukraine knows about Bitcoin, and most have Bitcoin accounts. They're the fourth-highest peer-to-peer users of Bitcoin in the world.

Citizens in Belarus have also woken up to what Bitcoin can do for them. The country monitors and tracks 100% of the monetary system. Every asset, every piece of property, account, and transaction is scrutinized by the government. They regularly freeze funds and put citizens in jail if they receive any support outside its borders. They effectively operate as if they already have CBDCs with complete control over how and when people can spend their money.

Over half the citizens in Mexico have no bank account whatsoever. 67 million Mexicans live on the currency they can physically carry. It's one reason Mexican Senator Indira Kempis is attempting to make Bitcoin legal tender in Mexico.

The remittance market in Mexico is over $150 billion. Many families receiving these payments belong to the poorest socioeconomic sectors of the population. But to avoid the 9%+ consumed by intermediaries and companies to get that USD into Mexico, citizens are turning to Bitcoin.

Almost $52 billion of that $150 billion activity is remitted using Bitcoin. Each transfer costs anywhere from 2 cents to fractions of one penny when sent on Bitcoin's rails. No middlemen. No censorship. Value retains integrity during its travel on Bitcoin's monetary rails. And settlement is instant and final.

Turkey, Iran, and Cuba are just some of the many other countries migrating to Bitcoin. Say what you want about their governments, dictators, or politics. Citizens who disagree want a way out. They don't have a choice when legally barred from currencies outside their fiat. And the hyperinflation levels keep them from investing in or supporting their own country.

Over 40% of Brazilians and Indonesians own Bitcoin. About 35% of those in Singapore and the U.A.E. own Bitcoin. In the U.S., about 20% of Americans own Bitcoin. However, the U.S. as a nation holds more Bitcoin on their balance sheet than any other, with over 200,000 Bitcoin.

The fact is that authoritarian regimes don't have a reliable currency for people to store their life's capital, their hard work, and their time. Whether censored, sanctioned, or inflated away, people have no freedom when they don't have their own money or are told how to spend it.

Bitcoin removes broken money because it separates money from state.

We already have a worldwide opt-out system called the internet. It's a public system for anyone to communicate regardless of government or restriction. People figure it out.

But the only open public system the world has for money is cash. Everything else is permissioned, regulated, and censored. So you're forced to use cash. But what choices do you have if you live in a country where that cash is consistently debased?

Bitcoin is the first globally accessible money and doesn't need a trusted intermediary, most of which, in these other countries, can't be trusted.

If you are against Bitcoin, you are against the people of the world.

Mr. Krugman, I'm sorry you think Bitcoin is "pointless and worthless." And Mr. Gates, I'm sorry you think Bitcoin "doesn't add to society." I ask you to take a look beyond your walled garden of privilege. Bitcoin wasn't created for you. Yet you too can benefit from it.

21

PROOF OF MONEY

"There is not the slightest indication that nuclear energy will ever be obtainable."

Albert Einstein, 1932

Hopefully, the last 20 chapters helped you understand Bitcoin better. For this final chapter, I summarize some of Bitcoin's main value points and how it fits in your future.

Bitcoin removes permission.

No one should be able to take away your money. The money that you have earned and worked for is yours. It is a tool to carry your excess value forward into the future.

No one is in charge of Bitcoin, so there's no permission to be granted. And there are no users in Bitcoin's system. There are only addresses with public and secret keys. That is all Bitcoin sees.

Bitcoin is proof of work and code. When anyone uses a calculator, the calculator only cares about math, not the person. If Bitcoin knew who you were, even a nickname, it would know too much.

Bitcoin only cares about sending and receiving value as securely and inexpensively as possible without any intermediary or third-party restriction. It does this without fear of a double-spend, counterfeiting, or supply increase.

Bitcoin removes secrecy.

Bitcoin is so transparent and truthful that it is on an open ledger for anyone worldwide to copy, download, verify, and validate. It is so blatantly honest it can't hide if it wanted to.

Banks, companies, and governing bodies have the same access and control as you. There's no VIP platform, premium software, backdoor code, state-level access, admin key, or root version of the system.

Everyone has the same tools and records because Bitcoin only knows addresses and keys.

If a company offers services around Bitcoin, those are *their* services. They interact with Bitcoin no differently than you. It's why self-custody is essential.

Bitcoin is not secret, but it's private. You shouldn't have to reveal your home address when buying a taco from a food truck. We are so accustomed to revealing the last four digits of our social security or showing our driver's license that we don't question it.

Bitcoin removes discrimination.

It is the most inclusive form of technology we've ever had. It doesn't care if you're toxic or have integrity, if you're judgmental, self-righteous, a bad person, or Gandhi.

Bitcoin doesn't care if you're wealthy or poor. It doesn't care if you're a company or a country. Everyone on the planet is equal in Bitcoin's eyes. It treats everyone equally regardless of race, religion, sex, wealth, or status.

Fiat's outdated technology doesn't protect war refugees, dissenters, activists, or the disenfranchised. It is incongruent to be against Bitcoin if you are for human rights. Bitcoin can't know your education, career, income, politics, or debts.

Bitcoin avoids human bias so that no one can be excluded. Anyone who uses Bitcoin does so voluntarily and usually out of necessity. With Bitcoin, we have global money that is fair and egalitarian. No one can be canceled or de-platformed for using Bitcoin.

Bitcoin removes monetary theft.

Now is the first time in human history we have given property rights to 8 billion people all at once. No one needs to get in line. The opportunity is here right now.

Anyone can have control of their own property. There's no counterparty risk with a bank to hold the note, a government to inflate its supply, a county to place a lien, a company to split the stock, a bond to default, or even someone to peer in your window and see your Bitcoin.

Most have never experienced this type of self-sovereignty. Bitcoin is a massive innovation of technology that any humanitarian can appreciate. Everyone can enjoy the benefits of rights and value.

Bitcoin is deflationary money - it prices goods and services with lower prices over time. Your time grows in value rather than depletes. You could save your stored time rather than gamble with it. You could work less on things you dislike and more on things you like. Deflationary money makes life more fulfilling.

The number of people who can participate in Bitcoin is infinite. Eventually, just 1 Satoshi will be pretty valuable, so there is plenty for everyone.

Bitcoin can't be taken away.

Governments can make it challenging to own Bitcoin but can't ban it. They can limit on and off-ramps, raise capital gains taxes, and restrict traditional banks with regulation. However, just as the internet has officially been banned in many countries, there is no country without the internet.

For a government or bad actor to take your Bitcoin, they would have to take down every single node in every continent, in every country, in every city, in every house, apartment, and basement, including those in the middle of the desert in an RV running via a satellite connection.

There is no single point of failure with Bitcoin. Its security is in the nodes disbursed all over the world. And its strength is in the shield of electricity created by the miners. This genius setup is integral to understanding Bitcoin's value as a monetary system that can withstand any imaginable force.

On top of this, thousands of Bitcoiners use TOR browsers and VPN internet connections that hide their actual location. A nation or state can't stop what it can't find.

The government can go after Putin. It can go after a CEO, a politician, or the face of anything. But Bitcoin's only face is the aggregate of every user looking in the mirror. This ever-growing network makes Bitcoin's proof of work stronger than the government's proof of force.

Militaries can be stopped. Courts can be stopped. Governments can be stopped. Bitcoin cannot be stopped.

The Streisand Effect says the more you try to ban something, the more you call attention to it. People learn of it and let facts speak for themselves. Gold, alcohol, and marijuana have all been banned. All 3 of those are everywhere in the world, and much more so because they were once banned.

Bitcoin is a technological improvement.

Much like the internet, Bitcoin allows peer-to-peer communication and free access to information globally with the same frictionless ability to transact.

As repetitive as it is to hammer this home, Bitcoin has a programmatically fixed supply. This fact cannot be overstated. It's so mathematically obvious that anything of value must be finite in quantity. History has proven this.

Everyone can account for the exact flow of new money and budget accordingly. This predetermined and auditable issuance level could never be altered to benefit anyone.

We will die without oxygen. It's one of the essential elements to sustain life. Yet because it is abundant, it's essentially worthless as money. Michelangelo's David is one-of-a-kind. But we don't need that statue to survive. Even so, it is so scarce it is worth hundreds of millions.

Engineers laughed at Thomas Edison when he said every household would have a light bulb.

Horse breeders said cars would never work since they break down and get flats.

Journalists depicted populations tangled and hanging in telephone wires when the landline was introduced.

The CEO of Microsoft laughed at the first iPhone, saying it was a huge business failure since there was no keyboard.

Critics laughed at the Wright Brothers' "toy that would never have real value" when they flew their first plane in 1903. Yet less than 60 years later, we sent humans to space.

Some don't see what Bitcoin can be because people fail to study history.

Bitcoin removes friction.

With Bitcoin, one can take $1 or $1 trillion across oceans or air, regardless of jurisdictions or flags, and in a split second at the cost of pennies. It is portable with zero weight or delay to move and transact.

Bitcoin is durable.

It can't decay, rust, melt, or dissipate. It has been called generational wealth because time can't stand in the way of Bitcoin. Grave diggers can't dig it up. It doesn't need maintenance or upkeep. 400 years from now won't make it any more difficult to access your Bitcoin than right now.

Bitcoin is location agnostic.

Having more or less doesn't take up more or less space, just as writing the number 9 versus the number 4 requires no more ink or paper. But paper will crumble, and ink will fade. Math, however, is forever.

Bitcoin is immutable.

It can't be undone, edited, or rescinded by anyone, including you. Unlike bank wires, credit cards, or checks, Bitcoin has finality. There is no ambiguity about who has the value and when it left one person and went to another.

There is no escrow with Bitcoin. Middlemen and associated fees are unnecessary, redundant, and therefore non-existent.

And as obvious as it is, Bitcoin is natively digital. You can't physically hold it, and there isn't a representation of it in the metaverse. When you self-custody it, you own its original digital form, not a virtual replica of something else.

Bitcoin removes slavery.

Freedom is the most important thing in the world. It's why America exists and other countries' citizens want to be here.

For over 200 years, everyone has risked their lives to come to America because it's "free." Only some people make it. But for those who do, what happens when they're forced into payday loans and high-interest rates on top of inflationary debasement of our currency?

Governments that want to solve immigration issues aren't looking at the problem from the perspective of money. It's all about the money. That's why people flee their countries.

Bitcoin allows people to remain where they already are and gain the sovereignty they travel far to seek. If people could securely store and freely transact their wealth without inflation, many wouldn't need to flee in the first place.

Bitcoin removes politics.

Current monetary systems in fiat are entirely politicized. It's why citizens have their accounts frozen for thinking or believing a certain way. There is no freedom to be an activist or think against a government policy. And as nations go into debt, they inflate without votes.

Satoshi's objective was to depoliticize monetary systems. He did this by solving decentralization and setting up rules of math rather than rules of politicians. Bitcoin is politically agnostic but mathematically religious.

If you are a Republican or conservative, you want Bitcoin because Bitcoin is about individual accountability. It's about ownership and responsibility. It's on you. Bitcoin encourages free enterprise and strong defense.

Bitcoin is impenetrable as an alternate finance system immune to inflation. It has the most robust defense of any technology that has ever existed. And if you want to secure borders, the irony is to allow others the same freedoms of money you already have.

If you are a libertarian, you want Bitcoin because Bitcoin is free from any government control or influence. No one can tell you how to hold or what to do with your Bitcoin. Sure, they can, but you don't have to listen.

You have complete autonomy and thus responsibility for your actions with your money. There's no backstop, Federal Reserve, FDIC insurance, or anything to save you, just as libertarians want it. You save yourself with Bitcoin.

If you are a Democrat or liberal, you want Bitcoin because Bitcoin is owned and run by the people. It was created for the people in the first place. It is the Occupy Wall Street movement but without guns, death, and imprisonment.

There's no corporation benefiting from Bitcoin by standing first in line to receive it at the expense of others. Bitcoin flips the money funnel upside down. Individuals can more easily download an app and immediately buy Bitcoin than a corporation that needs charter approval, a board meeting, and shareholder votes.

Bitcoin directly improves social justice. It's the fairest form of global money. Bitcoin becomes the welfare for the needy, poor, and disadvantaged. It provides economic equality so that people can seek access to healthcare and education no matter where they are. Bitcoin is for civil rights and liberties, which should align with liberal values.

And if you're an anarchist, politically agnostic, or hate the world, you want Bitcoin because Bitcoin is the definition of disruption. It is bold, loud, striking, and unapologetic. It is anti-company, anti-government, and anti-capitalist. It supports the freedom to protest and challenge authority without fear of persecution.

Bitcoin removes violence

There is no need to defend Bitcoin with a military. Bitcoin is its own defensive technology, secured by Proof of Work's consensus mechanism. It converts energy into an army that can't be defeated. It allows everyone in the network to be the "military."

Bitcoin makes it more expensive for a nation-state to go to war to extract wealth from its citizens than participate in the world's fastest-growing monetary network.

If The Fed can't avoid printing fiat, they should print as much of it as possible and transition to Bitcoin. This will ensure the U.S. has monetary might in the future, as the opportunity is now available to any nation. It's like weapons of the future are just sitting there for the taking. Which nations will armor up?

Bitcoin's opportunity is equal, but its outcome is not. Some nations or individuals will learn and act on Bitcoin. Others will sit on the sidelines. Like anything else in life, it takes work. But with Bitcoin, everyone is allowed to work. And it takes the same amount of work whether you're Joe Blow or Vladimir Putin.

In the future, taxes can become the income source of nations, as legally intended. Taxes are supposed to be the cash register for governments. But they've mistaken the printer as their point of sale.

Governments can run their affairs like you have to run your household within budget. And votes can be required rather than misuse of the money printer.

Because the world's various fiats are inflating into infinity, Bitcoin will be history's most widely used monetary asset. Give it time.

With Bitcoin, you don't have to put on a facemask, put on a bullet-proof vest, or march all day holding cardboard signs. You can simply exchange fiat for Bitcoin. Each dollar that leaves fiat is a vote against this mismanagement of human action.

With the destruction that is happening around the world, people have had little choice but to rebel and riot, risking death and imprisonment. But now, they can choose Bitcoin as an option. We can all support this by also choosing Bitcoin.

Bitcoin unsubscribes from the state system without affecting anyone other than those who think they can control everyone. Those people lose impact as others depart and join a fair and hopeful alternate system.

Almost all of the issues we have with money have come down to the limitations of humans. And humans corrupt money.

For those who want to protest and stand for something, I assume they stand for better morals and ethics. You can only improve the world's morals and ethics by fixing the money.

Bitcoin helps the environment.

A bank of the brain can replace trillions of dollars and almost incalculable amounts of energy waste spent on the banking industry and red tape.

Bitcoin removes greenhouse gasses from the environment. It craves the toxic and pollutive CO_2 and methane already emitted directly into the atmosphere from polluters.

Almost any industry or process creating waste can be an energy source for Bitcoin miners. Bitcoin doesn't need an ounce of additional, new energy created for it. It will gladly take energy allocated to someone else they are throwing away.

Bitcoin can only survive with waste. There will always be waste from other energy users. In return, Bitcoin will give people money with integrity and sovereignty.

You will hear a lot of FUD and criticism of Bitcoin. Here is how I address those concerns with the misinformed:

You are right. Bitcoin is for criminals. It's for everyone. So is the internet.

You are wrong. Gold is not better than Bitcoin. Gold is the past. Bitcoin is the future. Bitcoin doesn't uproot landscapes. It is portable, divisible, fungible, verifiable, recognizable, and ultimately scarce. Gold is not. Gold is the horse carriage. Bitcoin is the car.

You are right. Bitcoin is volatile, as every technology has ever been during the first two decades of its existence. Assets discover their price while people figure out how new technology fits into their life.

You are wrong. Bitcoin is not too expensive. This thinking is a fallacy of unit bias. Bitcoin's price is irrelevant. What matters is that Bitcoin appreciates over time at the same rate for someone holding 1,000 Bitcoin or .00001 Bitcoin.

You are right. Bitcoin can be copied. Over 450 altcoins were all derived from Bitcoin, either flat-out copied or forked into a slight change. But users ultimately decide as all of these other coins are worth but mere pennies.

The English language, Wikipedia, and the Happy Birthday song can also be copied. Will others follow a new version or stick with what works? The Lindy Effect says the longer a technology survives, the more likely it will continue into the future.

You are right. Bitcoin isn't backed by anything. Rather it is backed by the largest, most decentralized army in the world of users who ensure a ledger abides by the rules of math. It's backed by the proof of work of everyone who wants to secure the value of their work.

Bitcoin is the scarce thing from which value is derived. Bitcoin backs itself.

You are right but also wrong. Bitcoin has no utility. It can't do anything outside of being the best money we've ever had. Its only use is to be money. Period. For that reason, it has value. But feel free to use bananas instead since those have utility and Bitcoin does not.

You are right but also wrong. Bitcoin is dependent on the internet. However, it also works without the internet. Bitcoin can operate entirely on satellite systems, shockwave radio, SMS, and mesh networks that people use in parts of the world.

In the event of a complete apocalypse, Bitcoin can even function by passing thumb drives back and forth.

You are wrong. Bitcoin is not a Ponzi scheme. A Ponzi requires a centralized company or person to collect new investors to pay off old ones. There is no counterparty in Bitcoin. There's no CEO or company to benefit from this scenario. Bitcoin promises no returns, minimum investments, or memberships.

Others regret not learning and buying Bitcoin earlier, so dismissing it as a Ponzi is easier. Companies can be Ponzi schemes. Bitcoin cannot. And Bitcoin doesn't need companies.

Crypto is filled with scams. But Bitcoin is not crypto. Crypto is just the blockchain version of everything we already have and know with traditional and legacy finance, stocks, and startups. Bitcoin is an entirely new universe.

This magical, almost inconceivable money now exists among us. There is irrefutable evidence that it can't be stopped. And it will eat up every money and currency in its wake that doesn't hold up to the values and principles that define pure, sound, and hard money.

Bitcoin is proof of money.

If you have any questions, I'd love to hear from you.

Email: tman@bitcoinblockbuster.com

Instagram: @ProduceYourself

Twitter: @ProofOfMoney

Author Bio

Emmy-nominated producer Terence Michael has produced over 20 movies and 30 TV shows. He owns a production company, a mortgage business, and consults entrepreneurs on how to cultivate their skills and strategize investments.

As a recovering real-estate junkie, he has flipped, rehabbed, and monetized all types of real estate from single family homes to multi-unit apartment buildings.

His 2017 self-improvement book, *Produce Yourself*, highlights the lessons that story teaches about optimizing the internal hero. And how to apply that to business and leadership.

His 2020 traditional finance book, *Make Bank (when you think like one)*, focuses on passive income strategies to earn higher interest rates with crowdfunding, fractional lending, and other accredited investor arbitrage opportunities.

This 2023 Bitcoin book, *Proof of Money*, reveals a superior, alternate money universe that is more fair and egalitarian than the traditional one, such as the one outlined in *Make Bank*.

The easiest way to find him is on Instagram @ProduceYourself, on Twitter @ProofOfMoney, or via email: tman@bitcoinblockbuster.com

Acknowledgments

Those who are part of my personal life know who they are. I am forever grateful for their support, patience, and love.

So rather than list my friends and family for typical egotistical reasons, I thought I'd highlight some people who continue to sharpen my understanding of Bitcoin. Some of their facts, figures, and observations have found their way into this book through my synthesis of "aha" moments.

3Blue1Brown runs a YouTube channel that explains Bitcoin's technical aspects with easy to digest animated videos.

Lyn Alden is a macro investment analyst with a background in electrical engineering. No one understands macroeconomics better than her. Her articles and newsletters are both a finance and economics masterclass.

Daniel Batten is a climate activist and VC tech investor. He was once a hardcore Greenpeace warrior against protocols like Bitcoin mining. But after academic research, he switched to becoming a loud champion for Bitcoin's ability to drastically reduce greenhouse gasses and encourage the build-out of renewable energy.

Robert Breedlove has a unique background in accounting, finance, and philosophy. If you crave deep thinking about money's historical implications on the human race, he's the philosopher you seek.

Jeff Booth's book, *The Price of Tomorrow*, is the best resource for understanding how technology naturally fosters a deflationary environment. Without directly writing about Bitcoin, Jeff wrote about Bitcoin.

Vijay Boyapati wrote an article, which has since become a book, *The Bullish Case For Bitcoin*. Because Vijay's writing was the first published information about Bitcoin I ever read, it remains pivotal for me. Vijay breaks down the qualities of, and compares, Bitcoin with gold and fiat.

Troy Cross is a Fellow at The Bitcoin Policy Institute and Professor of Philosophy at Reed College. He applies his academic and philosophy skills to help others understand energy as it relates to Bitcoin mining. If you want a kind and smart voice in your head, put on some Troy Cross from any podcast.

Alex Gladstein is an activist and leader at The Human Rights Foundation and Oslo Freedom Forum. He's the Bitcoiner with a heart of gold. He brings Bitcoin's tools to developing nations and disadvantaged people who need Bitcoin way more than you or me. He helped me understand just how privileged we are, and why it's easy for us to forget how money enslaves most of the world.

Evan Hatch is a developer and software engineer who has extensively researched the history and background of who the real Satoshi Nakamoto may be.

Arthur Hayes is an entrepreneur and founder of one of the first successful crypto exchanges, BitMEX. Although he's run into banking troubles and contributed to crypto's rise (rather than Bitcoin), he consistently puts out wicked-smart articles on macroeconomics and world-changing orders that ultimately favor Bitcoin.

Peter McCormack has the most downloaded Bitcoin podcast, *What Bitcoin Did*. He's a regular guy with regular questions. But he manages to attract the best thought leaders, entrepreneurs, and disruptors in Bitcoin's space. His podcast is a great one-stop hub for Bitcoin personalities.

Guy Swann's *Bitcoin Audible* podcast is my favorite and first go-to (even before Peter). Guy's claim to fame is having read more about Bitcoin than anyone on the planet. And he's probably right. The best articles either for or against Bitcoin end up here. And if like me, you prefer to listen than read, this is a great resource.

Michael Saylor needs little introduction. He's a billionaire, entrepreneur, and engineer. He runs the first publicly traded non Bitcoin company, MicroStrategy, to put large sums of Bitcoin on its balance sheet. Since then, he has built free Bitcoin education classes and seminars. And he continues to help other publicly traded and institutional companies adopt Bitcoin. Do yourself a favor and search "Michael Saylor and Tucker Carlson" interview. That's the video to show your parents.

Ross Stevens, CEO of Stone Ridge, wrote a letter to his shareholders in 2020. It's the most inspiring article I've ever read on Bitcoin. I knew I would write this book after reading it. Find it. Read it (or listen to it on Guy Swann's podcast).

Adam Wright, co-founder and CEO of Vespene Energy, is on the forefront of turning methane into Bitcoin by dropping miners onto city landfills. Until I learned about Adam's business model and research, I never thought about how much methane leaks into the atmosphere from our garbage, and how Bitcoin mining fixes this.

Fidelity Investments put out a thoroughly researched paper, *Bitcoin First: Why investors need to consider Bitcoin separately from other digital assets.* As its title implies, this report speaks to legacy finance institutions, and helps identify why investors need Bitcoin while also avoiding crypto. For the boomer curmudgeons who think Bitcoin is a scam, read what the largest and one of the oldest American financial institutions has to say.

There are easily over 30 other amazing Bitcoin educators out there – too many to name. And there are dozens of other Bitcoin books. Truth be told, I haven't read them (or finished them). Why? I purchased my first three Bitcoin books in 2018 from the most prominent authors in the space at the time, but I couldn't get through them. I found these books dense, tedious, and in some cases too technical for me. I didn't feel the authors were trying to educate but rather display knowledge. Yet, those books remain popular in the community, so it's my issue not theirs.

Many say to write the book you want to read. And that's mostly why I wrote this book. It's the book I wish I had (and desperately needed) when I first heard about Bitcoin. Its culmination is in no small part thanks to those listed here.

Epilogue

I have a small request to make: please give this book a rating on Amazon or wherever you purchased the book. This link will take you directly to the review page: linktr.ee/terencemichael

Believe it or not, when it comes to books, reviews are highly impactful for other readers. It's an SEO and algorithm thing. I wouldn't ask if it didn't move the needle. But it really does.

Thank you, in advance. I respect your time. I will personally read anything written, so I appreciate any reaction you have to the book.

Follow me on Instagram @ProduceYourself, Twitter @ProofOfMoney. Or email me: tman@bitcoinblockbuster.com

Good luck. And keep stacking Sats!

www.ingramcontent.com/pod-product-compliance
Lightning Source LLC
Chambersburg PA
CBHW030454210326
41597CB00013B/665